SUNRAYS OF SOLACE

By

JOE M. MARTINEZ

ACKNOWLEDGMENTS

My success in life did not come by without the help of some wonderful people that came into my life. Some were in my life for a short while and others for a longer while, but each one of them helped in my being successful.

Great love to my parents who did the best they could considering living circumstances and hardships. To my Mother, who was such a positive person in my life and inspired me to persevere. I will always remember her unconditional love she had for her children and grandchildren.

Thanks to my wonderful son, David, my wonderful daughter, Nelda, my wonderful daughter-in-law, Jackie and my grandchildren, Ashley, Michael, Meghan, and Madison, for their love and caring. Thanks to my great-granddaughters, Crystal and Alicia and to Felipe, who will soon be part of our family.

Thanks to all the people that encouraged me throughout my growing up years and through my life. Thanks to my high school English teacher, to my head nurse at Hendricks Hospital, to Annie Hidalgo and Stephen Langley, who helped in encouraging and in completing the publishing of this book, and to all my wonderful friends, who are too many to name.

Thanks to all who encouraged me to write my life story. I love each and every one of you.

Thanks to George O'Neal, my partner, who has also encouraged me in writing this book and for being patient with me. I love you.

And last, but definitely, not least, to C.D. Burrough, who encouraged me and almost physically carried me to college to continue my education. Without him, I would not be where I am today. I miss you, love you and someday, I will see you again.

TABLE OF CONTENTS

SUNRAYS OF SOLACE
INTRODUCTION

As I started to think about my life, I thought about my parents and their lives. I was thinking about the stories my Mother would tell me about her life and I remembered how much I enjoyed listening to her. I found her life story very interesting even if I had already heard the same story several times before. When I started thinking about my Father, I realized I did not know anything about him. I realized my Father had not told us anything about his life growing up or about his family. He never talked to us about his parents. I did not know my Father's family, especially his parents.

I thought about my grandchildren and great-grand-children and what they would remember about me. I started thinking about my life and decided to allow myself to share my life with my children, grandchildren, and my dear friends. In sharing my life, I have shared parts of my life that I have often talked about and I will be sharing parts of my life that I have never shared before except with the psychologist. I have opened the door to my life with the hope that those dear to me will see it as this being my life and not cause any ill-will towards anyone. If sharing my life helps someone, may it be a parent or child, then sharing my life was well worth it.

I have being sharing parts of my life story with my children, grandchildren and with my very close and special friends and with those that I have met and have had only a short friendship relationship with, such as co-workers, neighbors and acquaintances. Several of those friends and acquaintances encouraged me to write about my life, as they felt it was interesting to them.

Hopefully those that have already heard some of my stories will not find it redundant and boring in reading this book, but instead, find it interesting and hopefully will feel that they know me better.

In writing about my life as I can remember it, it will be just that, simply my life. These writings are not meant to arouse anger from any one person or persons or race.

What I have written is true and only what I can remember, some things very vividly. I did not write this to put people down or make fun of people. I did not write this to arouse awareness of what happened years ago with the Hispanic people. Nor is it meant to depict how badly some white people treated the other races. It is not meant to point out racism in any way. I wrote everything that I can remember, as accurately as I can remember, so that my grandchildren and great-grandchildren will know where their grandfather came from and how he came to be who he is.

CHAPTER 1

MY PARENTS

It seems that most people who pen their autobiographies usually start back in time when life was poverty and hard work. And I guess I will not be any different.

My Father was tall, slender, dark brown skin and bald, with little hair on the sides and the back of his head. He always wore a baseball cap except when he dressed up, and then he would wear a dressy type, felt hat. The only time my Father would remove his cap or hat would be when he sat at the table to eat. If he forgot to remove his hat, my Mother would quickly remind him to show respect to the Lord at the table. My Mother also would not allow us men to sit at the table to eat if we were not wearing a shirt. Our shirts always had to be buttoned up.

My Father liked to kid with people, but only if he knew them well. He enjoyed making us laugh. Even though he enjoyed kidding with us and his friends, my Father was really a quiet man. He would sit for a long time without talking, just listening to the radio or staring into space. He would sit on the porch and watch the cars drive by. Occasionally someone he knew would drive by and he would wave.

My Father was a hard worker. He did labor work all of his life. He worked at ranching and labor work in the fields. He did not speak English, but understood well enough to be able to do the work. My Father was good at shearing sheep and he was able to make the most money doing that kind of work. He was strong and fast and therefore able to shear more sheep. But the problem was, sheep shearing was only in the fall and the spring. The rest of the year, my Father did very little work. He picked cotton, chopped cotton and did a few odd jobs here and there. He would often help the farmers out in the fields or work with the city picking up the trash.

Even though, my Father was a hard worker, he happened to be a negative person. He would quickly give us reasons why we could not do something we wanted to do. I often wondered if he became a negative person because of us being poor. We never had the money to buy what we needed or wanted, so he may have thought if we did not have money, we could not do anything.

My Mother was born out of wedlock. Her mother, Isabel, had become pregnant by her married cousin. After my Mother was born, Isabel married a man with the last name of Aguirre. Isabel died giving birth to a child. Mr. Aguirre then told my Mother that he could not afford to raise her, so she was sent to live with her biological father. My Mother was a small child about 5 or 6 years old at the time.

My Mother found out that she had four stepbrothers and six stepsisters. She never talked to me about her brothers and sisters after she went to live with them. I assume they loved her as their sister because later in life, they visited each other and were happy to see each other. I do know my Mother loved her brothers and sisters.

My Mother used to say that her father was very authoritative, mean and the children would get punished if they disobeyed him. Because he had problems with one of his legs, he had to use crutches to walk. His problem with his leg eventually got worse and, as my Mother described it, it sounds like he developed gangrene and died.

She told us about the time she was fourteen or fifteen years old. A girl friend had given her a note from some boy. My Mother got the note and put it in her pocket. She did not know that her father had been watching. Her father called her to come in to see him and he asked what she had in her pocket. She handed him the note and after he read it, he raised his crutch over his head and hit my Mother between her shoulders. Soon after that my Mother went to live with her Tio Pancho (Uncle Frank).

At the age of 15 years old, Tio Pancho, brother of my Mother's mother, Isabel, brought her to live with him and his wife and children. The suffering continued. Tio Pancho's wife now had my Mother as a live-in baby sitter and house maid. My Mother would baby sit when Tio Pancho and his wife would go out. My Mother did the laundry for the whole family using a rub board.

My Mother was hanging clothes on the clothes line when my Father walked by the house. He saw her and they visited for a short while. My Mother said she was afraid that my uncle and his wife would come home and see her

talking to my Father or anyone. My Mother was sixteen years old at the time. A few months after they first talked, my Father walked by the house and my Mother was again hanging clothes she had washed. My Father knew the situation with Mother and her uncle's wife, so he asked my Mother if she would marry him. My Mother said yes, and they ran off, eloped.

The next day my Mother and Father came by the house to pick up my Mother's clothes. My uncle's wife had packed all of my Mother's clothes in paper bags and had them ready for my Mother to take with her. My Mother and Father would be living near the house where my Father's parents lived. My Mother said that when she took her clothes out of the paper bags, her clothes had all been cut to shreds. Tio Pancho's wife had gotten angry and had used the scissors to cut my Mother's dresses. Mother said she did not care. She said that she and my Father had lived very poorly, but that my Father was very good to her. She used to tell us that my Father had taken her out of hell. My Mother always used to say, "We have lived very poor, but your Father is a good man."

My Mother was a short woman, four feet eleven inches, to be exact. As far back as I can remember, she had always been plump with a very gentle, kind face. She smiled often and when she laughed hard, her whole body would jiggle. She wore short wavy black hair that became a beautiful gray later in life. She had a light complexion and was a pretty woman.

She was a loving mother and showered her grandchildren with love and attention. Her many friends respected her and loved her for her kindness and caring. If one of her friends was sick, my Mother would go visit the sick friend to see what she could help her with. With the visit, she usually would bring some sweet bread she had baked.

My Mother was a great cook. She made the best flour tortillas and refried beans. Because we never had enough money for candy, cookies, cakes and other sweet breads, she would make snacks that we felt were better than store bought treats.

My Mother, unlike my Father, was a very positive person. She would always tell me that I could do anything I wanted to do, if I wanted to. My Mother was a hard worker. Everything that we had was because of my Mother's positive attitude and hard work.

My Mother was a very good seamstress. She would sew dresses for my sisters and made them look exactly like the dresses in the Sear's or Montgomery Ward catalogs. She would do sewing for the girls in our little town to make extra money. She would also do ironing for some families. She would also work in the fields chopping cotton or picking cotton.

All her life, my Mother gave us children a lot of tender loving care. The best part is that her grandchildren got to know her, spend time with her and feel that special unconditional love she had for them. My Mother's positive attitude, her great unconditional love that she showed towards me and her belief that I could do something special in life helped me to become successful in my life.

CHAPTER 2

NOVEMBER 29, 1945

I was born in 1945, in the private home of a cousin in Eden, Texas. I was supposed to have been named Josemaria, after my Father's father. The name Josemaria is a common Spanish name, but the name is written as all one word. No space between Jose and Maria. My birth certificate has me down as Jose Marie Martinez. My high school diploma has my name as Joe Mary. I am known by the people from Melvin by my nickname, Chemo. My driver's license has me down as Joe Martinez. My social security number has the name Joe M. Martinez. Go figure.

I grew up in a small central Texas town by the name of Melvin, Texas. Melvin had a grocery store (the Red & White), two gas stations, a post office, a bank, a café, an animal feed store and a lumber yard. Melvin's population was maybe around eight hundred people. The people who lived in Melvin were either white or Hispanic. We did not have any African Americans in our little town, or as they were referred to, Negro or colored. Growing up, I realized that the same racial prejudice by the white people that applied to the African Americans also applied to the Hispanics, or as we were referred to Mexicans.

My family and I lived in a long, old army barrack that was divided in half, into two large rooms. One side of the army barrack was where my parents, my three sisters and I lived and the other half of the barrack was where my uncle, my Father's older brother lived by himself. Apparently, my uncle had bought the Army barrack and the lot it sat on. My parents moved in with him. My Father's brother had never married. He had served in the Army during World War II and after the war, he had come to Melvin and bought the property.

My uncle was a quiet man, or so people thought. He meddled into our lives. He would tell on my sisters and Dad would get after my sisters. My uncle seemed to get a kick out of that. You can guess how my sisters felt about it. My Mother cooked, washed and ironed his clothes. Once a year she washed his blankets and quilts and he never gave my Mother a dime. He would give my Father seven dollars a week. That was for all the hot cooked meals he got, the laundry, and the groceries. My Mother never complained. Some relatives from my Father's side of the family thought that we received a lot of financial assistance from my uncle. I know that none of the relatives would have done the work that my Mother did and not get paid. At least, no one volunteered to wash, iron, and cook three meals a day for him.

We had two regular size beds on one side of the one big room that we considered our home. My parents slept in one

bed and my three sisters slept in the other. I slept on a metal framed cot. In one corner of the room, on the side near
the beds, was a closet that my Mother had made. She had
nailed a three foot long two-by-four board on the ceiling
and one on the floor. She then used cardboard and brown
wrapping paper to close in one side of the corner where she
had nailed the two-by-four boards. She then used a wire as
the hanging rack that went across the inside of the space
that was to be the closet. The closet door was a curtain that
my Mother had handmade. At least this paper closet kept
the hanging clothes hidden from view when friends would
come to visit.

On the other end of the big room was a dining table, refrigerator, stove, and kitchen counter. This area was considered the kitchen. This one large room was our home until I
was well into my teens.

The barrack had no sheetrock on the walls, only the
bare wooden boards. It did have sheetrock on the ceiling.
The outside of the barrack was covered with asbestos sheets
that were of the same material as roof shingles are made
of. The roof of the barrack was covered with tin metal that
sounded extremely loud when we had a hard rain or hail.
The windows of the barrack were large windows that would
slide to the side to open. The breeze would come in through
the windows and kept us very comfortable during hot days
and at night while we slept. We never had air conditioners
or fans.

Winters in the old Army barrack were damned cold.
Since the barrack did not have any sheetrock, it did not
have any insulation. We had only one small gas space heater in the one big room and the kitchen stove to keep us
warm. The space heater was lit at five in the morning in

an attempt to warm the house by the time we were to get out of bed. My Mother would wear a sweater when she was cooking in the kitchen. My Mother would light the oven and keep the oven door open so she could warm her feet.

I remember I would tuck my pants and shirt under my blankets next to my body to warm them up so that I could put them on. Once the pants and shirt were warm, I would put them on while still under the covers and then I would get out of bed. I slept with socks on to keep my feet warm.

My three sisters slept in one regular size bed which helped them to keep each other warm. My youngest sister would sleep in the middle, so she never complained of being cold. My two older sisters each slept on opposite sides of the bed. Quite frequently my two older sisters would get into a tugging match with the blankets, each claiming the other had a larger part of the blankets. The arguing would get loud and continue until my Father would get upset and threatened to "get his shoe".

My Father would often get a shoe and tap them on the head to make them stop arguing. My sisters usually knew the shoe thumping was coming so they would cover their heads with the blankets or place the pillow over their heads. The next day, they would laugh about the shoe thumping and who got thumped on the head the most. My Father would not thump them hard enough to hurt them. He just wanted them to keep quiet so that we all could go to sleep.

At night we all went to bed at the same time. When my Father was ready to go to bed, we all had to go to bed. Lights had to be out. Since there was only one big room, none of us could stay up late. Once we got into bed and the lights were turned off, we all would start saying good night to my Mother. I guess kind of like the "Mexican Waltons," except we were all in one big room instead of in separate rooms in a big house. Once we said our prayers to ourselves, we would say "Hasta manana" (until tomorrow) and my Mother would answer , "Si Dios quiere"(With God's will). If there was to be a blanket tugging match between my two older sisters, it would occur after every one said good night.

We did not have inside running water. For drinking water, we would have to carry a pail of water from the out-side water faucet. The water faucet was a few feet outside the barrack. We did not have to carry the water bucket too far, yet we all would fuss about whose turn it was to go refill the bucket. We maintained a dipper in the water bucket and we all used the same dipper to drink water. We were not concerned about diseases or germs or think of it as "yuk". My Mother would maintain a clean cloth over the water bucket at all times.

In cold, freezing weather, a thin layer of ice would form in the bucket on the surface of the drinking water. My Father and my uncle would cover the water pipes outside to keep them from freezing. Sometimes, the pipes would freeze and my Father would thaw the pipes with hot water. But the pipes would not freeze that often and they never did burst.

Since we did not have running water inside the barrack that meant we had no bathroom inside. We had an outdoor toilet or outhouse as we called it. I will not go into too much detail about the outhouse except that when it was cold, we usually would hold off going to the bathroom (or outhouse in this case) until we could no longer keep from going. Then we would run to the outhouse as fast as we could, and get out as quickly as we could. This practice oc-curred in cold weather only.

Because we had no running water, that meant we had no shower or sink. We had a washtub made out of galvanized metal and a bucket that was used for us to carry water for bathing. We used my uncle's room for bathing. We would let everyone know, especially my uncle, who lived by himself in the second large room in the army barrack, that someone would be taking a bath. That meant that no one was to enter the room until the all clear signal was given. Whoever was going to take a bath would fill the bucket with water and place it on the stove to warm. We would use the galvanized washtub that we would get into and use a cup to pour water on ourselves.

After the bath, we were responsible for throwing out the dirty water and cleaning the bath area. When the "all clear" signal was given, my uncle would go back to his room. We bathed three times a week and Sunday night was a "for sure" bath night. We had to be nice and clean for school on Monday morning.

Meal time, whether it was breakfast, lunch or supper, was a fun time for the whole family. My Mother would cook for all seven of us (that includes my uncle) and we would all sit at the table and eat together as a family. The food was always very good even though we usually did not have much to eat. We had refried pinto beans at every meal. Sometimes that was all we had to eat. But even if pinto beans and flour tortillas were all we had to eat, we still sat at the table as a family.

My Mother would make fresh flour tortillas for every meal time. As a snack, my Mother would get a fresh tortilla, put butter on the tortilla and give it to me. The only other person that can make tortillas as good as my Mother could make them is my youngest sister. My youngest sister can cook as good as my Mother and seems to enjoy cooking as much as my Mother did.

During winter, food became very scarce. My Father was a laborer and during winter there usually was not much labor work. My Mother would iron clothes and sew dresses for other families in order to help put food on the table. I remember that on several occasions, my Mother would send my older sister and me to the Red & White grocery store to ask Mr. Stewart if he would allow us to get groceries on credit. Mr. Stewart was the owner of the Red & White grocery store and would give credit to families that lived in the small town of Melvin.

I hated to go ask for credit because I was the one that had to ask and I was always afraid he would say no. But Mr. Stewart would always smile and say, "Sure, I will put it on your bill," as if it was my bill. My sister and I would get whatever groceries my Mother had told us to get and go home happy because we knew we would be eating well for the next few days. In the summer we would work out in the fields and pay Mr. Stewart the money for the groceries. He would wait several months for the money and did not tack on interest. This type of kindness does not exist anymore.

We, as a family, were coffee drinkers. As far back as I can remember, even when I was in the first grade, my Mother would place a cup of hot coffee at the table for me to drink while I ate my breakfast. We all drank coffee at every meal. My Mother would use the same coffee grounds to make coffee until the coffee would be too weak. She would then throw out the coffee grounds and use some new coffee grounds.

We usually ate eggs for breakfast every morning. If Old Grandfather did not give us any eggs, we would buy eggs at ten cents a dozen from a little old man and his wife who lived a few blocks from where we lived. As many eggs and beans as I ate growing up, eggs and beans are still my favorite foods.

I was the third oldest child and the only boy in the family. My parents had a son, who would have been the oldest, but he died as an infant. I do not know what he died of, but to hear my Mother talk about my brother's death, I think it was crib death. The baby had been born healthy and was doing fine, but was found dead in his crib.

My Mother had six babies that were stillborn besides the four of us that survived. I remember the last stillborn baby my Mother had. The baby girl was a big baby for a new born. I remember seeing the baby, but I was young and did not really pay too much attention to what was going on. I do not remember going to the funeral for my baby sister. All I remember is seeing the baby lying on a table, dressed in a white dress, not moving or breathing, just lying very still.

Being the only boy in the family, people thought, and frequently would say, that I must be very spoiled. I was not and do not feel I was raised spoiled. In fact, it was the opposite. I had to work, and maybe work harder because I was the only boy in the family. We were very poor. Being very poor is one of the things that my sister, Emma, and I remember and talk about the most.

We at one time owned a car that had to be hand cranked to be started. I was very young but I remember that I had to crank the car and once it started, I would place the iron crank gadget in its holder above the front bumper and then I would run and get in the car. Occasionally my older sister would have to crank the car, but usually I was the one that had to get the car started.

CHAPTER 3

FIRST GRADE

Melvin had a small school which housed students from the first through the twelve grades all in one long brick building. The first grade class room that I attended was located behind the long brick building. It was separate from the brick building. It housed the first grade only for the Hispanic children and the third grade which included both Caucasian and Hispanic children.

The first grade was divided into two sections. The first two rows were first year first graders and back two rows were the second year first graders. The second year first graders were the Hispanic children like me that had to repeat the first grade. The Caucasian first grade children were in a separate room that was part of the long brick building where all the other children attended school. In this present time and age, this would not be allowed, as

15

it would be considered segregation and racist. But at that time, it was allowed and it was considered the norm for the Hispanics.

I do not remember my exact age or the exact year, but I remember when I was in the first grade. I do not remember the first day of school when I started first grade. I only remember being in the first grade. Like most of the Hispanic children, I did not speak English when I started school. The only English I spoke was "Joe Martinez."

I enjoyed going to school. I learned the alphabet, learned words, and I learned to put the words together to form a sentence. It was rather difficult for me to learn to speak English. Once I got out of school in the afternoons, it was back to speaking Spanish. No one spoke English at home nor did I with any of my friends. If I spoke English when I was around my friends, they would make fun of me, teasing me that I wanted to be a "gringo." So the only opportunity I had to learn English was at school.

My first grade teacher was a large, tall (at least from where I was looking at her), older gray haired woman who wore her hair up in a bun (as I remember it being called). Mrs. S. wore round wire rim glasses with bifocals. I remember how she seemed to have her head raised up when she read. It always looked like she was looking at us instead of at the book. Now I realize that she was reading through her bifocals, as I have to wear bifocal glasses now.

Mrs. S. wore black shoes that laced up in front and had short, stumpy heels. Because she was overweight, the heels of her shoes would stomp loudly when she walked on the hard wood floor. Many times, she would intentionally stomp on the floor to get our attention or if she was upset with one of the students.

Every day Mrs. S. would bring an old record player/radio to the school. We would play records and sing along to children's songs until it was about 8:45 and then it was time to listen to the local news from the nearest local radio station in Brady, Texas. The local news lasted about five minutes. The names of all the people who were admitted to or discharged from the Brady hospitals would be announced along with all the deaths. Our class would begin after the local news.

I do not remember Halloween or Thanksgiving when I was in the first grade. We were migrant workers and were usually up in north Texas working in the fields picking cotton until all the cotton was picked. Usually all the cotton was picked by the end of November or the first part of December. At that time we would pack our belongings and drive back to Melvin.

During Christmas in the first grade, we decorated the Christmas tree, colored Christmas pictures and sang Christmas carols. We would make Christmas decorations out of paper and each student would hang their own hand-made decoration on the tree. Every morning I would walk up to the tree and look at the decorations as if it was the first time I had seen them. We never did have a Christmas tree at home. We did not have the money to buy the decorations for the tree.

On Christmas day, my parents placed an apple on my pillow. When I woke up, I was very excited to have gotten an apple for Christmas. That was all that my parents could afford to do for us at Christmas. We only got a small stocking filled with candy once or twice that I can remember. But an apple was a great present for me.

My most memorable time in the first grade was at Easter. Mrs. S. had each one of us make a rabbit out of two

17

small paper sacks. Each student was given two small brown paper sacks and one cotton ball. We stuffed a wadded piece of paper in each small brown paper sack to make the paper sack expand. We then wadded the open end of one sack and scotch taped the puckered end as tight as we could. Next we stuffed the puckered end into the other open paper sack and then wadded the open end of the outer paper sack. We taped the outside of the bag to form an "hour-glass" with the two small paper sacks.

After that we cut out two long triangular pieces of paper that we had colored pink. We glued each triangular piece of paper to two corners of the top paper bag to form the ears. We drew two eyes, a curved line to form a smiling mouth. Next we cut three long skinny pieces of paper that we had colored black and glued them above the curved line that formed the smiling mouth. Now we had three long whiskers.

The last thing we did was cut two triangles that we colored using our favorite color. Mine were blue, because blue has always been my favorite color. We taped two tips of the triangle in the middle of the two paper bags where the puckered part was. We had just created a little rabbit wearing a bow tie. Finally we glued the cotton ball to the back of the brown paper sack that was considered the lower part of the rabbit's body. The rabbit now had a fluffy cotton tail.

We each were required to tape the rabbit on the front of our desk. We were instructed that our rabbit was to be kept there until Easter. I can still remember how we created the little rabbit, and in my mind, I can still see the little rabbit staring at me.

I remember the spelling class and how we were required to learn the alphabet and read words written on the blackboard. There was a long small bench up against the wall under the blackboard. The small bench was placed under the blackboard so that we could step up on the bench and reach the blackboard to be able to write.

The teacher would go to the blackboard and choose a word for us to learn. As an example, I will use the word "CAT". She would write the letter C, and then say C sounds like the letter K. The A sounds like Ah. Then we would say the letter T several times. Then we would all have to say K-ah-t. CAT, K-ah-t. CAT. She would pick students at random and have the students go to the blackboard. She would then pronounce the word CAT. She would then say C. The student was to write the letter C. If the student did not know how to write the letter C, the teacher would write the letter C on the blackboard. This would be done on each letter until the word CAT was spelled out.

If a student had difficulty spelling out the word, the teacher would become angry. She would then get the "learning board" that she used for paddling. If the student still had difficulty with a word after the teacher went over the whole C-A-T process, she would then swat the student one time for each time that the teacher explained and the student was still not able to spell CAT. The student would get up to three swats. After that the student would have to sit down. Trust me, there was never a time that I had difficulty learning to spell.

I remember when I received three swats with the "learning paddle" due to my not being able to speak English to defend myself. The third grade white girls would play ball behind the building that housed the first and third grades. The girls would have the boys run after the ball. Normally we stayed away from that area during play period because we would get tired of running after the ball. On this particular day, some of the boys were in that area and had refused to run after the ball. The girls reported to Mrs. S. that the boys were fighting with them.

When we were inside the class room, the teacher asked the boys to raise our hands if we had been playing behind the building. Not one boy raised his hand. The teacher asked a second time. She then told us that if we did not say who was fighting with the girls, we would all get a paddling. I did not know who had been playing in that area. Because we would not say who was fighting with the girls, the teacher had all of the boys circle the long tables that we used as desks.

The teacher then sat at one corner of the long desk with the paddle. She made us walk around the tables. As each one of us walked past the corner where the teacher was sitting, she would swat us with the paddle. If a boy tried to run past her, she would have him walk back and receive his swat. We all got three swats. Needless to say, after that, we made sure to run after the ball or completely stay away from that area. I preferred to stay away.

CHAPTER 4

OLD GRANDFATHER

Our next door neighbors were Hispanic families that were all related. The families included the Old Grandfather, the Old Grandmother, four sons and three daughters, all of whom were grown and married. The Old Grandmother and the Old Grandfather lived in a little one bedroom house next to the ally.

In the next house on the same lot lived the second oldest daughter, her husband and their two daughters. Catty corner across the road to the daughter's house lived the oldest daughter, her husband and six children, three boys and three girls. Next door to the oldest daughter lived the second oldest son with his wife and two girls and a son. The other three sons lived in the same town but several blocks away.

The children from each family, including my sisters and me, were in the same age range. There was about a seven year difference between the youngest and the oldest. We all were friends and used to play together. Sometimes we used to fight with one another. The anger would last but only a few minutes and we would all be playing together before the end of the day.

My Mother would put the leftover food from our plates into a two gallon can that we used as a slop bucket to feed to the hogs. I would then carry the slop bucket to Old Grandfather.

Old Grandfather was a short man, about five feet three inches tall, bow-legged, bald and always wore a dirty felt hat. His pants were baggy and he always wore old, brown, worn-down work boots. He had a grey mustache, sparse hair, and a scratchy, short beard. Old grandfather smoked cigarettes and his clothes smelled of smoke. Old Grandfather was the grandfather to all the children I was friends with and played with.

Old Grandfather always had farm animals in his back yard. He had at least two cows that he milked every evening. He would share the milk with his children and with the neighbors, including us. He had chickens and pigs, and the slop that I carried over to his house would be fed to the pigs. I would help him feed the chickens and fill the pots and pans that he had on the ground for the chickens to drink water.

Next, I would then fill the troughs for the pigs to have water to drink. After all that was done, I would place the water hose in the large vat that was filled with water almost daily for the cows to drink. After I helped him do all that work, he would give me some eggs to carry back home and a jar full of fresh milk. I was always proud to take the milk and eggs home because I knew that sometimes it was hard for us to afford to buy milk and eggs.

I enjoyed the animals. I would sit by the pig sty and watch the pigs eat. Sometimes the pigs would bathe in the mud and I would watch, fascinated by the way they enjoyed the mud.

The chickens would peck the ground constantly. I often wondered if they actually ate something each time they pecked on the ground, or just pecked the ground in the hopes of getting something to eat. I tried to get the chickens to eat out of my hand. I was able to get a chicken to eat out of my hand at least once or twice. The chickens were too skittish. They would run off flapping their wings at the slightest movement I made.

Gathering eggs was a great enjoyment for me. I loved the smell of hay. Walking around to the places where the chickens would nest to lay their eggs and the smell of the hay was the best part of helping Old Grandfather. He always warned me about snakes, but I never saw a snake. Even now, I can still remember the smell of the hay.

The day was a cool, clear sky day in the late afternoon. The sun was shining as I filled all the proper containers with water for the animals to drink. I saw Old Grandfather carrying the fresh milk and eggs into his house. He then came back to where I was finishing with the work. He sat the paper sack with the eggs and the jar of milk on a wooden bench that he had under a tree next to a fence.

As he sat the eggs and milk on the wooden bench, he told me to follow him into the old wooden house that he used to store the hay and feed for the chickens. I followed him into the old house. I could see the sun rays shining through the cracks between the boards. The old house did not have outside siding or inside sheetrock. It was just the wooden boards that were left of an old house that may have been livable at some time.

Old Grandfather closed the door and placed an old board across the door locking the door from the inside. I stood in the middle of the one room storage house, listening to the quietness on the outside. Old Grandfather smiled as he walked towards me. I was wearing striped overalls and Old Grandfather started to unbutton the metal buttons on my striped overalls. I began to feel very uncomfortable. I knew that what he was doing was wrong and he should not be doing that. I backed away as he undid one of my buttons. He told me not to be afraid, that he would not hurt me as he unfastened the other button to my overalls.

I could smell the horrible odor of cigarette on his breath and his clothes mixed with the odor of sweat. I felt my overalls slide to the floor. I looked at the wall and saw the sunlight shining through the cracks between each board. I faintly heard him unbuckling his belt as he started touching me. Out of fear and not knowing what to do, I focused on the bright sunlight shining through the cracks between each board.

All was quiet, too quiet. I could hear the sounds of the pigs as they ate, the chickens clucking as they pecked on the ground eating whatever grain was left on the ground. I could see the sun rays come through the cracks and they looked like I could almost touch them. Some of the sunrays made very straight lines of different widths. Some of the boards had holes of different shapes and sizes. I looked at the different shapes of sun rays shining through.

I felt Old Grandfather pull my clothes up and button my overalls. He smiled at me and stated, almost as if in a question, that I would not tell anyone what had just happened. He went on to tell me how my parents would punish me. He told me that my parents would use the belt on me.

I walked back home not knowing what I should do. I could not understand exactly what had happened, yet I knew it was something that should not have happened. Older men do not do that to little boys. But why did Old Grandfather do that to me? What had I done? I felt dirty. And I felt extreme fear. I felt like anybody could just look at me and know what I had done. I was afraid to go home.

When I walked inside our house, I thought my parents would punish me. I felt like as if they already knew I had done something bad. I remember standing at the door inside our one room barrack home and not moving. My Mother asked me where the "slop" bucket was. I realized then that I had forgotten to bring the slop bucket back with me. I heard my Mother say that I needed to go back and get the slop bucket. I couldn't move. After what seemed like hours, but I am sure it was a few seconds, my Mother opened the screen door and motioned for me to go get the slop bucket.

Just then, I saw Old Grandfather at the fence that divided his and his daughter's property from ours. He was smiling, telling my Mother that I had left without his knowledge and that he meant to send some eggs and milk. I walked over to the fence, very hesitant about getting too close to Old Grandfather. Once I got the slop bucket and the bag with eggs and a jar of milk, I hurriedly walked back to the house, so sure that he would come from behind and touch me. But my Mother was standing there holding the door for me to come inside. My Mother thanked Old Grandfather and she closed the door behind me. I felt safe once I got inside the house and the screen door was closed behind me. That night, I slept with my clothes on. I did not want to touch my own body. I fell asleep.

Morning time was the usual start of day. My mother started the coffee, lit the oven and started breakfast. I was informed that it was time to get up and get ready to go to school. I got up, washed my face and brushed my teeth. I needed to go to the bathroom. I dreaded going to the bathroom in the outhouse. Once I stepped inside the outhouse and locked the door behind me, I started experiencing fear. The wooden boards of the outhouse let the light in through the slits between the boards. I began to think about what happened the day before. What happened yesterday evening was my fault. I must have done something to cause Old Grandfather to do that to me. I was bad and I needed to go to church. Maybe if I did not think about what happened. And so in my mind, I focused again on the sun light coming through the boards.

My usual routine was for me to walk to school after I ate breakfast. Since school was only one block away, my sisters and I walked to school unless it was raining. Even in cold weather or snow, I walked to and from school. If it had snowed, I would play in the snow all the way to and from school. I never did mind having to walk.

But today was different. Walking to school, I kept looking back to make sure Old Grandfather was not following me. There was a small pasture, about half a block long and the neighborhood children and I would walk through the pasture via a small lane we had created walking to and from school. We all felt it was a short cut to get to school. Today, I walked along the side of the road instead of the short cut. I was afraid to walk through the pasture. Once I got to the school and closed the class room door behind me, I felt safe.

School started in the usual way, with the teacher listening to the morning news and then class started. After school, I rushed home and stayed inside. I pretended I was studying. Slop day was only two or three times a week, so it would be one or two more days before I had to carry the slop bucket to Old Grandfather. I played with the neighborhood friends, Old Grandfather's grandchildren, but I made sure that I stayed away from any place that Old Grandfather might be. I came home early when it was still daylight and made sure I was inside the house when it was dark. My parents were always busy and my two older sisters were usually with the two sisters next door (Old Grandfather's granddaughters). No one really noticed me and that was better for me because I was afraid that my horrible secret would be known.

Two days went by fast and it was time for me to carry the slop bucket to Old Grandfather. My mother had to call me several times before I eventually picked up the slop bucket and headed next door to Old Grandfather's back yard. I walked slowly not really knowing what to do. I remembered that last time I brought the slop bucket and what had happened. I would make sure I did not do anything that would cause Old Grandfather to do anything to me. That was it. I just would not do anything to cause him to touch me. I felt more comfortable about bringing the slop bucket to Old Grandfather.

When I finally reached the pig sty, I sat the slop bucket on the same old bench just as I had always done before. Old Grandfather smiled at me and gave me an old empty coffee can to go to the old house and bring some grain to feed the chickens. As I walked to the old house, I noticed that Old Grandfather was looking at me and smiling. I walked into the old house, quickly filled the coffee can with grain, spilling more grain on the floor than I had in the coffee can and hurried to the door. As I stepped out the door, Old Grandfather was sitting on the old bench next to an empty slop can.

As I brought the coffee can I had half filled with grain, Old Grandfather motioned for me to sit next to him. I stared at him as I slowly sat where he had motioned for me to sit. He patted me on my head as he placed his arm around my shoulders. He looked at me and asked me if I had said anything to anyone about "us playing" inside the old house. Immediately all I could think of was seeing the sunlight shining through the old boards and holes in the wall of the old house and the many shapes made by the sun.

He then told me that I must not tell anyone because I would get into trouble with my parents. "Your parents will use a belt and you know how much that hurts. So you must not tell anyone," he said as he stood up and handed me the empty slop bucket. He then smiled at me and told me to go home and be a good boy. I ran as fast as I could run, not looking back. I was elated that nothing had happened. I was right, nothing would ever happen again.

Even though nothing had happened with Old Grandfather, I ran as fast as I could, just in case. Once I was inside my house I felt safe. The screen door closed behind me and I turned around and looked across our yard, across the fence to where the pig pens were located. Old Grandfather had finished feeding the animals and was walking to the back door of his house carrying two cans, one in each hand. I watched as he sat one can down on the back steps leading to the kitchen, opened the screen door, grabbed the can back up and walked inside his house.

As I lay in my cot that night, I thought about Old Grandfather. He did not do anything to me. Old Grandfather had not touched me. Maybe he would not ever touch me again. I felt like it was finally over. I did not have to worry any more. It was over. I said my prayers, said good night to my parents and fell asleep. I felt safe.

CHAPTER 5

MIGRANT WORKERS

As I have said before, we grew up very poor. I do not think that we were the poorest family in Melvin, but we were close to it. We were migrant workers who worked in the fields. Because we worked in the fields, our work was done in the summer and the fall. Money was very scarce from December to June. During the summer and into the fall, we would go to north Texas to work.

We worked in the fields chopping cotton (cutting weeds growing where the cotton plants were growing) from June to the end of August. Then we would pick cotton from September to the end of November or December. We also worked in the fields picking onions, carrots and potatoes, but this work only lasted a few weeks. We worked long, hard hours for very little pay.

At the end of the school year, we loaded our old car with whatever few necessities we could get in the car. The whole family piled into the car and headed to north Texas. Every year we would follow the same process as the year before. My Mother would pack all the kitchen pots, pans, dishes and utensils into a large, round, metal washtub. The washtub would be the first item to be loaded into the trunk of the car.

We did not have suit cases so our clothes were packed into cloth sacks. Blankets and quilts would be placed on the back seat of the car. Other odds and ends would be carefully packed on the floor of the back seat of the car. The mattress from my cot would be rolled up and placed on the floor of the back seat.

My Father would neatly pack everything in the trunk and back seat of the car so that everything we needed would fit in the one car along with my two parents and the four of us kids. Due to the mattress, blankets, quilts and other odds and ends on the back seat, there was only about two feet between the blankets and the roof of the car.

My Father would drive all the way to north Texas, which was about three hundred miles from Melvin, with my Mother sitting in the front seat next to my Father and my older sister sitting next to the door. My second oldest sister, my younger sister, and I would get in the back seat of the car and lie down for the long drive to north Texas.

My Father drove slowly due to our car being so old. The whole trip would take us most of the day. We would get up at 4:30 in the morning and be on the road before six. My Father always felt that if we would get to San Angelo before sunrise, which was about seventy miles west of Melvin, we would be making very good time.

The long drive to north Texas was a big challenge for my younger sister and me. You see, my next to the oldest sister would position herself on one side of the car and that was her space. My younger sister and I could not get close to her or touch her because she would get very upset. We were afraid of her and so the whole trip was us trying not to get near her. The best thing for us to do was sleep as much as we could. If we were awake, my younger sister and I would play games as best we could, but there was always pushing and shoving and my Father would have to yell at us.

There were two best parts of the whole trip. One was when we would stop at a grocery store to buy bologna, bread, Fritos and soft drinks. We would drive to a road side park outside the city limits of whatever town we happened to be in and eat. We really enjoyed the bologna sandwiches and we thought how wonderful it tasted.

The second best part was when we arrived at our destination. We were never sure where we were going. One year we went to Dimmitt, Texas, the next year to Hereford, Texas. We lived in so many towns in north Texas: Levelland, Littlefield, Spade, Plainview, Edmonson, Garden City, Taylor, Roscoe, Whiteface, and Flag, to name a few. But it did not matter which town we lived in, we were happy being there. Dimmitt, Texas, was our favorite town to go work. We knew some people there and we all liked the town.

CHAPTER 6

SECOND GRADE

This year we went to Edmondson, Texas, which is about fifteen miles northwest of Plainview, Texas. In Edmondson, we lived in a large tent out on a farm which seemed to be in the middle of nowhere. There were four of us families that lived in the tent. My aunt, who was my Father's sister, her husband, and their six to eight kids, and two other families that did not have as many children, lived in the tent. The tent was divided into four sections with two large picnic tables in the center. The picnic tables were used by all four families. We used kerosene stoves with two burners. We all slept in the tent. I was in the second grade at the time.

The smaller children went to school while the older school children and adults picked cotton. I was in the second grade at the time. The school bus would pick us up in front of the house where the owner of the farm lived. He and his wife were nice people who were kind to us. They had three children, one daughter who was the oldest, a son who was about my age and a young son who was not of school age.

Riding on the bus to and from school was not so bad. We, being Hispanic would have to sit towards the back. But we could not sit all the way at the back of the bus because the very back seats were for the black children. The bus would pick them up to take them to their school. The black children would attend a separate school from the school that I went to with the white children.

Being in the second grade I never gave it much thought to the African-American children going to a different school. It was common knowledge that the African-American people were not allowed in certain places and that they had to ride in the back seats of school buses or city buses. We had to sit towards the back but had to leave enough seats for the African-American children. Hispanics were not allowed in certain places either, so it was something we just accepted.

I remember taking lunch to school and eating in the cafeteria. My lunch was a potted meat sandwich with an apple and a nickel so that I could buy a small container of orange juice. I always thought that was a great lunch.

After school, all the children would be given a snack and then have to go help pick cotton. I would use a burlap sack and every time I would fill the sack with cotton, I would empty the filled burlap sack into my Father's 10 or 12 foot sack. As far as I remember, none of us children ever refused to go pick cotton. To us, working in the fields was a way of life. We knew that we had to work and we also knew that we could argue and protest all we wanted, but we would still end up having to go to work.

On weekends, the Hispanic families would go into Plainview and spend all Saturday afternoon and evening enjoying ourselves. On Saturday mornings we would all bathe, put on our best clothes, then load up in our old car and drive to the city to go shopping, to the movies, and in the evening, go to the dance. A large number of Hispanic families would park around the court house in the center of the city. There were stores all around the court house, two theaters, and a hamburger place that sold the best hamburgers.

Going into the city on Saturdays was very enjoyable for us boys. Once we arrived at the court house yard in Plainview, we would go to the movie theater. There were two theaters in Plainview, but only one theater would allow Hispanic people. With one quarter, I would pay ten cents to go in the theater to see the movie. With the fifteen cents I had left, I would buy a large bag of popcorn for five cents, a soda for five cents and a large pickle for five cents.

We would get to see two movies, cartoons and a continuing serial that would last about fifteen minutes and would leave us in suspense until the next Saturday, when we would find out if the hero got to save the damsel in distress. We would talk all week long voicing our own ideas as to how the hero would save the damsel in distress. It was all very exciting for us and we kept going to the movies every Saturday.

The other theater in Plainview that theater would not allow entrance for the Hispanic or African American people. I remember very vividly when theater was showing the movie Peter Pan with Mary Martin as Peter Pan. The second grade children were taken by the teachers to see the movie at the theater. The Hispanic children stayed in the class room while the white children went to see the movie. I got to see the movie with Mary Martin as Peter Pan for the first time in the 1990's.

I would sometimes ride back home from the city with my cousins in their large panel truck. The back of the truck had wood panels on the sides all the way around the back. A large canvas covered half of the back of the truck. There was a door at the tail end of the truck that opened inward and a ladder that we would drop down to allow people to climb up or down the back of the truck. I used to enjoy riding back home in the back of the truck.

My cousins and I would place blankets on the floor of the truck, grab pillows and lay down looking up at the stars. We would talk about the movies we had seen until we would all fall asleep. If the night was clear and not cold, our parents would leave us there all night. Other older boys would also sleep there on the truck. Remember we were living in a tent, so sleeping on the back of a truck was not that unusual. We had blankets to cover up with and if we still got cold, we would grab the cotton sacks that were left on the truck and cover ourselves.

One night, we had a big storm with strong winds and rain. The two poles inside the tent were swaying and the tent canvas made loud noises as the strong winds blew against the canvas. Some of the men were trying to hold the poles steady to keep them from being knocked down. But the wind was too strong. The tent slowly started to tear from the top at the site where one of the tall poles held the tent up. Within minutes the two poles were knocked down and the whole tent lay on the ground.

By that time, all of the people inside the tent had gotten into their cars and trucks to stay out of the rain. The winds soon slowed down and we were all able to get some sleep. In the morning, we all helped pick up all our belongings and loaded them into our cars.

The owner of the property was up very early and started to help in finding living quarters for all four families. We all found places to live near each other, maybe two to five miles apart. My family was relocated to a small wooden house that was being used as a storage place for grain. The small structure was divided in half by a wall going half way up to the roof. One side had grain and the other half was where we lived. It was a small half room, but we were glad that we lived in a "house". We felt safer here and it was warmer once the weather started getting cold.

We lived in Edmondson until the end of November, and then it was time for us to go back home to Melvin.

Towards the end of November or first week in December, all the cotton was picked and we started getting ready to go back home. I say the end of November or first week in December because I really do not remember exact months and days. I only remember that it was before Christmas because I made it in to the Melvin school to help with decorating the classroom Christmas tree.

My young sister and I would get all excited about going back home. We would gather our toys, coloring books, and whatever we had to use to entertain ourselves during the long drive home.

My Father woke us up at four in the morning and we helped carry our well packed belongings to the car where my Father would very carefully pack them into the car. Every bit of luggage had to be carefully placed to where all the items plus my sisters and I would be able to fit into the car.

My Father made sure that we were on the road no later than six in the morning. He drove all the three hundred or so miles without stopping except to fill the car with gas. Stopping to fill the car with gas was our opportunity to go to the restroom and stretch a few minutes. We would always arrive in Melvin and at our army barrack by mid-afternoon or early evening, all tired but very excited to be home.

Starting the second grade late in the first semester of the school year was not so hard for me. I already knew the kids that were in my class room, since most of the Hispanic families had returned from north Texas. My first day at school felt as if I had been going to school since the beginning of the school year. Different this year was white and Hispanic children attending school together. We also had a new homeroom teacher.

Mrs. M., my second grade teacher, was a very nice, sweet lady who had a sweet voice and did not frighten us when she spoke. While it was different having white boys and girls for classmates, we all seemed to get along very well in and out of the classroom. I enjoyed going to school.

The weather was mostly cold this time of year. If my Mother felt it was too cold for us to play outside, my younger sister and I would stay inside. If I would sneak outside to play, she would call me to "Come back inside or you will get sick.", unless, I was with my Father, and then I could be outside as long as I wanted.

My Father and the neighborhood men would meet at one of the men's house, light a fire and spend several hours talking, either sitting or standing by the fire. We (the boys) would go outside and play close to where the men were talking and keeping warm by the fire. If we got too cold, we would huddle by the fire and warm ourselves. When we had warmed ourselves up, we would go back to playing and keep repeating the process until the men would put the fire out and we would all head home.

I continued having to carry the slop bucket to Old Grandfather's hogs. I could not get out of having to carry out this chore. On one particular evening, I took the slop bucket as usual and helped him feed the pigs and chickens. We got through with all the work that had to be done and I helped him carry the large jar of milk into his house while he carried the eggs and whatever other things he had with him. Old Grandfather told me to place the large jar on the kitchen table while he placed the eggs on the kitchen counter.

He then asked me to come with him to the living room. His house had only one bed room and a living room with a bathroom and the kitchen. The house was "L" shaped and the side window in the living room was facing his daughter's house. His wife was at his daughter's house and his wife would wait for him so she could come back with him. She would not walk the small path that was only a few feet from her house by herself.

Old Grandfather sat on the couch and called me to come over to him. As usual, he was smiling at me and held his arms open for me to come to him. Suddenly, I felt him pulling on my belt. He kept telling me that he would not hurt me and that my parents would spank me if they found out.

Because I knew I could not keep this from happening, I was happy when I saw the sun shine brightly through the cracks of the boards. I found myself focusing on the bright sunrays, shining through the cracks between each board and all was quiet. I could see the fine sunrays come through the cracks and they looked like I could almost touch them. Some of the sun rays made very straight lines of different widths. Some of the boards had holes of different shapes and sizes. I looked at the different shapes of sunrays shining through.

I found I could block out all that was happening, even the horrible smell of cigarette on Old Grandfather's clothes by looking at the sunrays coming through the cracks between the boards of the old house.

I felt Old Grandfather pull my clothes up on me, button my pants and buckle my belt. I walked behind him as he walked the narrow path to his daughter's house. I had to walk the same narrow path to be able to go to my house. As we walked the narrow path he reminded me that my parents would be very angry with me if they found out what "I" had done. He made it seem as if it was my fault, my doings. He reminded me of how little boys get punished if they do bad things.

I walked inside the army barrack so afraid that my parents would know what I had being doing and that it was my fault. I slowly walked to my cot, wondering if my parents already knew what I had done. I sat down on my cot and listened, waiting to be punished. When my parents did not make any move to punish me, I slowly got up to walk over and sit down with the rest of the family to listen to the Spanish novelas (Spanish soap operas) on the radio.

My Mother would listen to the Spanish novelas every evening. This was a family event.   My Mother and Father would sit in front of the old wooden radio and my sisters and I would sit next to them forming a half circle around the radio. We listened intently to the novelas and talked only during the commercials. On most occasions, my Father would bring a sack of pecans and shell pecans while we listened to the novelas. We enjoyed eating the pecans that my Father shelled and drinking coffee. After the novelas were over, it was time to go to bed.

Next morning I got up and got ready for school. I ate breakfast and walked to school. I remember walking to school thinking I was such a bad boy. Old Grandfather had told me my parents would think that. I was a bad boy. It was my fault and I felt dirty and ugly.

At school I could forget about Old Grandfather. I did not have to think about what I had done or what had been done to me. My teacher was nice and made going to school fun. Once school was over, all of us that lived in the neighborhood would walk home stopping to look at something someone would see or discover, talk, play marbles or whatever other thing we would do until we got home.

When I would get home, my Mother would greet me with a smile and ask me if I wanted a snack. Since she smiled at me, I assumed she had not found out that I had been a bad boy. I played inside the army barrack. Again, I did not want to be where Old Grandfather could see me. One of the neighborhood boys came to see if I wanted to go play. I did not go play, I chose to stay home.

Today was the day for me to carry the slop bucket for Old Grandfather to feed the pigs. Again my Mother had to remind me several times until finally I slowly went and grabbed the slop bucket and headed to Old grandfather's house.

When Old Grandfather saw me coming with the slop bucket, he gave me a smile and stretched his hand out for the slop bucket. I barely lifted my arm to hand over the slop bucket. Usually the slop bucket was heavy and I would have to stop several times to rest my arms or change the bucket over to the other hand. I do not remember whether the bucket was heavy or not, whether I had to stop and rest or not.

I remember standing there after Old Grandfather fed the pigs. He handed me an empty slop bucket and told me to go home. I slowly turned to go home feeling as if he would come behind me. I turned to look back expecting something to happen. He was not following me. He had not taken me into his house. He had not touched me. I ran home as fast as I could run.

That night lying in bed, I covered my head and closed my eyes. I was afraid. It was dark and my cot was right by the window. Every time I opened my eyes, I could see straight out the window. I was afraid I would see Old Grandfather. I prayed and prayed until I fell asleep.

Several weeks went by with me carrying the slop bucket to Old Grandfather and I would come back without having to go with him into his house or into the old house used as a storage barn. I did not understand what was going on. Maybe Old Grandfather did not want to touch me anymore. I felt a great relief to think that Old Grandfather did not want to do that to me anymore. It was over, finally.

I still pulled the covers up over my head every night because I was afraid to look out the window. I was also afraid to turn over, facing away from the window because I felt I would be grabbed from behind. I would pray and pray until I fell asleep.

Christmas, New Years, and Easter had passed and it was getting close to the end of the school year. Holidays for me were uneventful due to the fact that we did not do anything differently than any other day. The holidays only meant that we had days off and I could play.

Since Melvin was a small town, the nuns would drive in from Brady to teach catechism classes to the children. Every Thursday I was required to go to catechism classes. My Mother would tell us to go to catechism class so we could learn to pray. My Mother loved the Lord and frequently talked to us about loving Jesus.

The nuns taught me how to pray. For that, I was very grateful because prayer helped me get through the nights when I caused Old Grandfather to sin. I still could not understand what I had done to cause Old Grandfather to do those things to me. And he was right in telling me my parents would be very angry at me if they found out.

The nuns would tell us there were two types of sin. Mortal sin was the worst type of sin and we go to hell with mortal sin. Venial sin was a lesser sin that would not send us to hell if we committed venial sin. If we died with venial sin, we would go to purgatory and suffer for our sins until we went up to heaven. We were taught that it was a mortal sin if we did not go to Mass on Sundays. I wondered if it was a mortal sin I was committing with Old Grandfather.

I learned fast about mortal sin. There used to be a Baptist church located between my house and downtown. The preacher "Mario" had come to our house inviting us to a birthday party they were having at the Baptist church. There would be cake, cool-aid, candy and balloons for the children. It was not that often that something that fancy was held for any Hispanic children that I had known, so I wanted to go and have some of those wonderful goodies the preacher had mentioned. So I went.

When the other children found out I had gone to the party at the Baptist church, they told the nun at the next catechism class. The nun looked at me and asked me if I had attended the party. I nodded my head indicating yes. I was instructed that I had committed a mortal sin and I needed to go to confession as soon as possible. I went to confession the following Sunday. Whew! That was close. I did not want to go to hell.

For the longest time after that, every time I had to go on an errand into town, I would run past the Baptist church instead of walking, afraid of the church and of committing another mortal sin.

Thinking I would go to hell if I missed Mass on Sunday, I would make sure that I went to church every Sunday. I had made my first Communion and now I could go to confession and receive Communion on Sundays.

When I went to confession, I would tell the priest about my not going to church, about my not obeying my parents, about fighting with my younger sister. But I held on to that one big sin. I could not tell the priest about that sin because I felt he would throw me out of the church. He could tell my parents and I would get a whipping. My parents would hate me.

And so I went on believing that I was going to hell. I had done an evil thing. My parents would probably not love me anymore. If other people knew, they would not want to talk to me. I would not have any more friends. And so I held on to my awful sin and kept on praying, hoping that somehow I would be forgiven.

Several months had passed and I continued to carry the slop bucket to Old Grandfather's. Old Grandfather had not touched me for those several months and I was beginning to feel safe. Everything would be okay now. Old Grandfather was not going to do anything to me anymore. Maybe even my evil sin would go away and I would not go to hell. I could see the light at the end of the tunnel, so to speak.

In May, the Hispanic families that my parents would visit or who came to visit with my parents would start talking about going up to north Texas to work. The end of the school year was only a few days away and the families that migrated to north Texas started preparing and getting ready for when school was out for the summer. I was excited because I enjoyed going to north Texas and I could get away from my nightmare. I could be at ease, knowing that I did not have to be afraid. I knew that I did not have to be bad. I did not want to be bad. I was looking forward to going as soon as possible.

One evening, towards the end of school, I brought the slop bucket for the pigs to be fed. After all the work was done, Old Grandfather asked me to help him carry the milk and eggs into his house. We sat the milk and eggs on the kitchen table and Old Grandfather went to the living room. Old Grandfather's wife was at her daughter's house.

The only light in the house was the light in the kitchen, but we could see into the bed room and into the living room. Old Grandfather smiled at me and motioned for me to sit next to him. I kept looking at the doorway leading into the bedroom and I could see the outline of the kitchen door on the bedroom floor. I found myself focusing on the bright sunlight shining through the cracks between each board and all was quiet. I could see the fine sun rays come through the cracks and they looked like I could almost touch them. Some of the sun rays made very straight lines of different widths. Some of the boards had holes of different shapes and sizes. I looked at the different shapes of sun rays shining through.

Old Grandfather handed me the old slop bucket and I rushed home as fast as I could. I kept feeling dirty and I could not understand why all this was happening to me. I was bad. I was doing bad things. I was sinful. I had made Old Grandfather do bad things. How could anybody like me? How could my parents love me if they found out that I was bad? I prayed and prayed until I fell asleep.

CHAPTER 7

THIRD GRADE

This year, I do not remember where we worked once we got to north Texas. I do not recall where I went to school for the first part of the semester in north Texas. I tried to remember something, maybe just one thing about the summer of this year, but I remember nothing. I only remember getting back home to Melvin and starting school in the third grade.

The third grade teacher was mean. I do not like to say that about my teachers, but this is an exception. She never smiled, wore wire rim glasses and had excess skin hanging under her chin. Every time she moved her head, the excess skin would move from side to side. She looked like she was very tall and she wore short stumpy heeled shoes. She was not over weight, but every time she walked, she stomped her heels on the wooden floor and you could hear an echo in the room. Every morning before she started class, she would pull a jar of mentholatum from her desk drawer, unscrew the lid, dig her finger in the jar and then place the mentholatum in her mouth. Then we would start class.

The third grade was uneventful. I was always afraid of the teacher, as were the rest of the Hispanic children. Nearly all the children that had been in the third grade under that teacher would talk about how mean the teacher was and how she yelled at the students.

The one thing that I remember from being in the third grade was that every week we colored a different flower and we placed the colored flower in a binder to save. There was a picture of a violet that the teacher had told us to color purple. I colored mine blue. I remember the teacher screamed at me and stomped her foot a couple of times as I stood there not knowing what to do. She finally pointed to my desk and told me to go sit down. I thought I had colored the flower purple.

Carrying the slop bucket to Old Grandfather was something that I felt was my punishment for being bad. I deserved the punishment. I had even lied to a priest. That was the worst thing a person could do. God would punish me like he punished my cousin. My cousin had argued with a priest and she told the priest to leave her house. Shortly after that, my cousin developed Bell's palsy. People at that time had not heard of Bell's palsy, but people would say that it was punishment from God because she had argued with the priest.

The times Old Grandfather touched me were not that often and each time it happened, I would focus on the old house wall, where I could see the bright sunlight shining through the cracks between each board and all would be quiet, almost peaceful. I could see the fine sun rays come through the cracks and they looked like I could almost touch them. Some of the sun rays made very straight lines of different widths. Some of the boards had holes of different shapes and sizes.

I looked at the different shapes of sun rays shining through. Somehow, in some way, that always seemed to help. I would not have to see or feel. It helped get me through whatever Old Grandfather was doing. I did not even smell the stench of cigarette smoke that permeated his clothes. The sun rays shining through the cracks was my solace. I would go into my world away from where I was and felt nothing, heard nothing and it saved me from the horrible nightmare.

When I got home, I quietly walked in wondering if this was the day that my parents would know I had done something bad. Once I realized my parents did not know anything of what I had done, I would relax and join the family in whatever it was they were doing for that evening. I was very afraid my parents would find out that I was bad. Afraid they would hate me for what I was doing. I wanted my parents to love me and if they found out that I was a bad boy, they would punish me and hate me. I had no idea how to make this nightmare stop. I did not know what it was that I was doing that was making Old Grandfather do those things to me. I wish I knew so that I could stop doing it. I would always pray until I would fall asleep.

CHAPTER 8

FOURTH GRADE 1956

The end of the school had finally come and now it was time to start getting ready to pack our mere necessities, load them into the car and go north. My Father woke us up very early and we all carried items to the car while my Father packed them neatly into the car. This time my uncle Jose was going with us. We also loaded some of our things into his car and he followed us all the way to north Texas.

This year we went to Flag, Texas for the summer. Flag, Texas consisted of a cotton gin and two long barracks divided into several rooms to use as housing for the migrant workers. This group of barracks filled with migrant workers was known as "campos" (camps). There were two houses next to the barracks that belonged to two Hispanic families that lived there permanently. The cotton gin, the barracks and the two houses were located several feet off the highway. By the highway was a small grocery store that was also a gas station. The grocery store/gas station was owned by a Hispanic man and his wife. The man had at one time lived in Melvin where his mother, brothers and sisters still lived.

I was not old enough to work in the fields chopping cotton, so I spent a lot of time playing with the other children that were my age or younger that got to stay home. I played outside most of the day and helped my mother with small chores. We still used a bucket for our drinking water. Maintaining the bucket full of water was my responsibility. The faucet for the water was outside next to the small building that was the shower room. Families from one barrack used this water faucet. The other barrack had its own water faucet.

When my two older sisters and my Father would come home from work, I had to walk to the little grocery store and bring sodas for all of us. I could not buy the drinks ahead of time because we did not have ice or a refrigerator.

My friends and I would use short pieces of two by four boards for toys. We would pretend the pieces of wood were little cars. We spent hours playing in the shade and only left our little playing area to eat or go to the restroom.

I walked around barefooted and wore shoes only to go into town. On hot days the ground would be too hot for me to walk barefooted, but I was instructed by my Mother to stay in the shade. If my Mother saw me playing in the hot sun, she would yell at me to come inside if I could not stay in the shade. I preferred to play in the shade.

On Saturday morning, we would all dress up and drive to Littlefield, Texas, to do the shopping. There we would meet one of my Mother's sisters and her three boys and two girls. I would hang around mostly with my Mother and my younger sister. Sometimes I would go to the movies while my Mother and sisters went shopping. I would be out of the movies by the time they had finished with their shopping.

By mid afternoon, we would head back home to el campo. Once we got home my Mother would prepare supper and I would walk to the little grocery store for the sodas. Even if it was on the weekend, it was still my responsibility to go get the cold sodas for us to drink.

After we ate our evening meal, my sisters would start talking about going to the Spanish dance. Every Saturday evening, the families living in the barracks would drive to Dimmit, Texas, about fifteen miles away, to attend the dance. If the parents of one family were not going to the dance, their teenage daughter or daughters would find a ride to the dance with one of the other families. Going to the Spanish dances was very important to the teenagers and not one teenage boy or girl would miss the dances unless it was due to sickness. Not one teenager got sick on a dance night that I know of.

The summer went by with the same daily routine, both during the week and on weekends. Weekends were more enjoyable because of going into town, to the movies, the dances and occasionally buying a toy. Store bought toys were not that common among the Hispanic children at el campo. We got pretty good at making our own toys out of whatever we could find, for example, making bows and arrows.

The bow was made out of a tree limb that was strong but yet could bend. We would cut a long thin string of rubber out of an inner tube from a bicycle or car tire. We would tightly secure the rubber string to one end of the tree limb and then bend the tree limb to form a bow. Once the tree limb was bent to the extent that we wanted, we would tie the rubber string to the other end. It would also work with a strong thin string or thin cord, but we discovered that with the rubber string, the arrows would go further.

The arrows would be made out of the stalk of tall weeds. I would remove the leaves, smooth out the stubs from the leaves and tie a nail at the heavy end of the reed. Once it dried, the weed would become sturdy and great to use as an arrow.

Slingshots were made out of a tree limbs that had divided limbs to form a "Y". I would use the same type of rubber string cut out a bicycle or car inner tube and strong string to tie the rubber string to the "Y" tree limb. We did not play with slingshots often because slingshots were dangerous. On several occasions, some of the boys had gotten hurt with rocks thrown with a slingshot.

In September, a few weeks before school started, we moved to Spade, Texas, a little town northwest of Lubbock, Texas. My Mother's sister, whom we met on weekends in Littlefield, lived on a farm near the little town. She and her husband invited my parents to stay with them and pick cotton there. We moved into a little house that had two small rooms that were about 12 feet by 12 feet. With the two small rooms, we thought we were in heaven. We were so used to all six of us living in one small room.

My Mother's sister and her husband (aunt and uncle) lived in a large three bedroom house with a living room and kitchen. Four of the five children were older than me. My aunt had a black and white television set and we often went to watch television at their house. I saw "The Wizard of Oz" with Judy Garland for the first time. There were about fifteen of us packed into one room watching the movie. There were wall-to-wall bodies sitting on the floor and chairs, as many as could get into the room without stepping or sitting on any one. We all talked about the movie for many weeks afterward, going over those particular scenes that we all thought were scary or funny or even sad.

My youngest sister and I went to school with my two younger cousins. I was in the fourth grade and I remember that I was quiet and shy. I usually stayed by myself during PE class. I would walk around the play ground and sit and watch the other children play.

The classroom had desks that sat two students to a desk. I got to sit next to a Hispanic boy that had difficulty reading or remembering his A,B,Cs. He was taller than me and had a larger body build. We started talking to each other and soon, I had a friend. We played football or other games by ourselves. Sometimes we even played with the other little kids.

The one thing I remember about him was how much he protected me. When we played football, he would not allow the other boys to be rough with me. He was constantly looking out for me. When we went to the cafeteria, he would make sure I had my lunch bag or made sure I could carry my own tray. He always made sure that there was a chair for me to sit next to him. When we played by ourselves, we always laughed a lot. It felt so good to be protected. I was very happy. I had never had a friend I had felt close to, a friend that protected me or just enjoyed being with me. I wanted this year to last forever.

All too quickly, it seemed, all the cotton was picked and it was time for us to go back home to Melvin. Normally I would be very excited when my Father would announce that we would be going back to Melvin early Saturday morning. This time I was not excited about going back home. I thought about my friend from school. I did not want to leave him.

When I told my little friend that we were moving back home, he was sad. I remember he gave me a little ball that we would often play with at school. I remember him saying, "I want you to have this ball." That afternoon when I got on the school bus, I sat next to a window so that I could see him and wave good bye. My friend ran to the school bus and kept waving and at times he would jump and tap the window where I was sitting. Then he ran to his school bus and I pressed my head against the window so that I could see him get into his school bus. He kept waving and I kept my face pressed against the window until I could no longer see his bus.

I did not cry, but I wanted to. I was hurting inside and I did not understand why. I did not understand why we had to leave. I did not understand why my friend and I could not continue going to school and sit next to each other, why we could not play together any more. On the way home on the bus, I felt sick, nauseous and I threw up. My younger sister, my cousins and I were always the last ones to be dropped off by the school bus driver, so there was no one there to see that I had vomited on the bus. I got off the bus and slowly walked the short distance home. Next morning, very early, we packed both my uncle's car and our car and we went home to Melvin.

The fourth grade in Melvin was okay as far as school went. The teacher was nice and again, I enjoyed school. My cousin, a son from another of my mother's sisters, and I were in the same class. Since we knew each other we began to play together in school. Even though I was friends with my cousin and the neighborhood boys, I preferred to spend much of the time by myself.

I continued to carry the slop bucket to Old Grandfather. Most of the time he would not touch me but on those few times that he did touch me, again, I would focus on the bright sunlight shining through the cracks between each board and all was quiet. I could see the fine sun rays come through the cracks and they looked like I could almost touch them. Some of the sun rays made very straight lines of different widths. Some of the boards had holes of different shapes and sizes. I looked at the different shapes of sun rays shining through.

Afterwards I would go home and pray hard until I would fall asleep. I was bad and I deserved being treated bad. I wanted my parents to love me and if they found out that I was a bad boy, they would punish me and hate me.

I missed my friend from Spade. I had a school class picture and I would look at the picture and think about my friend. I would fall asleep thinking about the two of us playing at the school ground, me chasing him and him letting me tackle him. He acted as if he was really running fast, but he would always let me catch up to him. I would think of us laughing. I would fall asleep.

At times I would think that if my friend was here, Old Grandfather would not touch me. My friend would protect me. He protected me at school and he would protect me now. But then I would think, if my friend knew what I had done, he would no longer want to be my friend. Maybe it was a good thing that my friend was not here. I did not deserve any nice, good friends. I continued to prefer to spend time alone.

The school year finally came to an end and again, we prepared to go up north to work in the fields.

CHAPTER 9

FIFTH GRADE

Going to north Texas we ended up going to Levelland, Texas where my Father's sister, her husband and children lived. There we rented a small one room little house that had at one time been used as a shed. The shed had been converted into living quarters located in the back yard of the property owned by a Hispanic family. Along with the little house was a shower located a few feet from the little house and it had hot water. I showered every day. You see, back then we bathed every other day or every three days. We had never had a real shower with hot water until now. We always used wash tubs to bathe in.

The little house also had a commode. We had always used outhouses. Most of the outhouses we used when we went to north Texas were community outhouses, used by all the people that lived in the campos. They were stinky and they all came with lots of flies. If you did not have a strong stomach, you would throw up and end up relieving yourself from both ends. Best of all, the shower and the commode were for our use only. We did not have to share with other families. We thought we were high class.

The summer went by too quickly. I had enjoyed living in the little house because of the commode and shower it had. Now my Father and my uncle were talking about picking cotton and talking about moving to a little town, sixteen to twenty miles west of Levelland. My Father, my uncle and my uncle's brother went and rented a two bedroom house, one bathroom and kitchen for all three families to live in.

We packed our car and drove caravan style to Whiteface, Texas. We got one of the bedrooms, where all six of us in my family slept. No big deal, we were used to having to sleep in one room. My uncle's brother and his family moved into the second bedroom and my aunt and uncle and their children moved into what was considered the living room. I think that is why they say Hispanics are clannish, three large families in a three room house.

The kitchen was shared by all. I do not know how we managed to eat during meal time. The children had to sit on the floor to eat. I do not remember how the kitchen was set up or how big it was, but there was a door that went to the back yard. The kitchen had to be pretty good size because my Mother, my aunt and my aunt's sister in-law were all overweight. All three of them would cook in the kitchen at the same time. I never heard of there being any fights between them!

And as for the bathroom, it seemed it was in use twenty four hours a day, seven days a week. There was little or no privacy. There would be constant knocking on the door by someone needing to use the bathroom. The men usually would use the bathroom at a nearby gas station. If I, or anyone for that matter, went out to the store, we would make sure that we used the bathroom before we came home.

School started in Whiteface, and those of us that were too young to pick cotton all day were sent to school. That first day, my little sister and I walked to the school not knowing where to go. I kept trying to find the office to register but we could not find the front office. My little sister started to cry. With me holding on to my little sister, we walked back and forth in front of the school building, until a young white lady came and asked us if she could help us. I told her we were looking for the office and we followed her as she walked us to the school office. My little sister was in the second grade. I got her registered and then I was told I would have to go to the next building to register.

I walked to the next building and walked to the office to register. I was in the fifth grade. After I got through with registration, I was escorted to the room that was to be my classroom. I got to sit at the very back of the room which was great for me. I knew no one there and I did not feel as if everyone was staring at me.

I do not remember anything about the teacher only that she was nice. I enjoyed art class. I remember drawing two butterflies and the teacher was very impressed with the drawing. My drawing was posted on the bulletin board in the hallway across from the principal's office. My name and class room number were written on the drawing. I never told my parents. My parents were busy and I felt they did not care or understand what it meant to me.

I also had to take music and I enjoyed that class. I have always enjoyed music and I wanted to learn as much as I could about it. Two songs that were popular then were "I Want to Walk You Home" by Fats Domino and second "I'm Just a Lonely Boy" by Paul Anka. We used to go skating on Saturdays and those two songs would be played several times while we skated.

Other than those two classes, I did not do much else in school besides studying. I was a loner and spent most of the PE class by myself. I would think about my friend from Spade, Texas, and wondered if he had found another friend. I knew I would never see him again. Being a loner, I had not made any friends. It would definitely be a lonely time for me here.

Every day after school, I would walk home with my sister and a cousin who was in the fourth grade. We would have to hurry home, change clothes and eat a snack. After we ate our snacks I, along with other school children, would be driven to the fields to pick cotton until it got dark. Also, most Hispanic school children that were in middle school and high school would miss school on Fridays to go pick cotton, unless it was raining.

Towards the end of November, the cotton was picked. We packed our car and started our cramped-in-the-car, tiring trip back to Melvin. Once we got to a certain location on the road that was about five miles from Melvin, we could see the water tower. As soon as we saw the water tower my little sister and I would start looking for our shoes to put on. My sister Emma would start combing her hair. There would be pushing, shoving and loud arguing until my Mother or my Father would have to yell at us.

As I have said before, my younger sister and I could not get too close to or touch Emma because she would pinch us or snap at us. But in the cramped back seat loaded half way to the roof of the car, it was very hard to keep from touching her or getting too close to her. We would calm down and just watch the water tower get closer and closer. Soon we drove through the downtown part of Melvin and a few minutes later, we drove in front of the barrack. We were excited about being back home again.

I started school right away after we got back to Melvin. My fifth grade teacher was nice. I always felt it was an advantage if the teacher was nice. Teachers that were not so nice did not understand my being "new" to the class. It would always take me a few weeks to get caught up with the class, but I did okay in catching up with my studies. I kept passing to the next grade with "C"s and sometimes if I got lucky, a "B" here and there. I studied at home but I did not have anyone to help me with my homework. My two older sisters had dropped out of school after the eighth grade. I did the best I could and worked hard.

I was growing up. I was getting taller and was developing into a young man. I still had to carry the slop bucket to Old Grandfather to feed the pigs, but things had changed. Old Grandfather was older and his wife was sickly. Old Grandfather started getting rid of his pigs and gave his cows to his youngest son who lived a few blocks away. Eventually all he had left was just a few chickens.

This year, Old Grandfather touched me only two times that I can remember. If I stayed away to where he could not see me or be anywhere near him, he would not bother me. I did a good job of making sure that I was not near him.

On this night, I had been watching television at Old Grandfather's oldest daughter's house. It had gotten dark and I walked the half block home alone. Old Grandfather was waiting behind an old shed that was used as a laundry room. He called out from the dark and told me to go with him. He instructed me to walk towards the old barn as he walked behind me.

We went inside and he closed the door behind him. He started touching me. I stood still knowing that soon I would see the sun shining through the cracks between the boards. Soon I would see the different shapes of sunlight shine through the different size holes in the boards of the old house. But this time I could not see the sun shine through the cracks between the boards. This time there were not different shapes formed by the sun coming through the cracks. This time there was only the awful smell of his cigarette breath, the smell of cigarette smoke that had permeated his clothes. Why couldn't I see the sun shining through the cracks, all different shapes? Where were my sunrays of solace?

I was cold, freezing cold. I wanted to get under the covers of my bed, cover myself up and go to sleep. But there was no bed. There was no one but me and this old man. I silently prayed, asking God to forgive me for all the sins I had committed. I asked God to forgive me for whatever I had done to be punished like this.

After it was all over, I walked home wishing and wanting everything that happened to go away. As I walked home I realized that it was actually a warm night.

I did not understand why this was happening to me. I did not understand why I feared this man so much. I had nowhere to go to get away from him and no one I could talk to. I would feel sick at the thought of telling someone. Whomever I told would hate me and would want to get away from me as fast as they could. Besides, all this was my fault and I deserved whatever happened to me.

One day I heard my neighborhood friends talking about the fact that Old Grandfather had gotten caught molesting one of his granddaughters. The granddaughter, who was about ten years old, had gotten a severe spanking. I actually heard the adults telling the granddaughter that she ought to be ashamed of herself. I knew that if my parents or anyone else were to find out about me and Old Grandfather, I would be punished just like the granddaughter. After all, it would have been my fault just like it had been her fault.

Old Grandfather was a short man of about five feet five inches tall. I kept telling myself that the next time he tried to touch me, I would beat him up and he would be afraid of me and never, ever touch me again. But that is not how it was. I realized that I was deathly afraid of the old man. I avoided him completely. Since he did not have any pigs, I did not carry the slop bucket to him anymore. Yet every time I saw him, even a few blocks away, I would experience that fear.

Avoiding Old Grandfather became easier as time went on. I began to spend a lot of time with my cousins that lived about a mile away. My cousin David and I were in the same grade and we had become friends. David, his brother, who was one year older than me, his two younger brothers and I would spend a lot of time together playing and taking long walks in the woods and along the railroad tracks. People would warn us about rattlesnakes by the railroad tracks, but even though we spent countless hours by the railroad tracks and the pastures, we never saw one rattlesnake. God was watching over us.

My cousins were poor like me. We had to create our own toys. We built little toy cars, wooden guns, and play houses. Our play houses were the most fun to build. We would find a space surrounded by little mesquite trees and then place cardboard on the inside area of the trees and secure the cardboard with wire. We would then gather tumble weeds and all other kinds of weeds and cover the cardboard on the outside. The little house would be large enough so that all five of us could crawl inside. If it was cold, we would build a fire to keep warm, but the few times that we build a fire, the smoke would drive us out of the little house. We never did figure out what we needed to do to keep the smoke from forcing us out of the little house. But we had fun.

I enjoyed spending time with my cousins. I did not have a brother or brothers, so spending time with them gave me the opportunity to do "manly" things or, shall I say, boy things. Having sisters was okay, but I wished I had a brother. Being around my cousins I learned to do alot of things that boys do, like making slingshots, playing Cowboys and Indians, wrestling, sleeping outside under the stars until we all got cold and went inside in the middle of the night.

My cousins would kill rabbits and my aunt would cook the rabbits for the boys to eat. I never ate rabbit meat because I did not like having to kill a rabbit. My cousins stopped eating rabbit meat when they developed lumps under their arms. When they went to the doctor, the doctor told them they had rabbit fever. I do not know whether the doctor really said that or if he did, if it was true, but my cousins never killed or ate rabbit again. I was glad I had not eaten any of the rabbit meat.

I spent so much time at my cousins' house that sometimes my Mother would send my older sister to bring me home. As soon as I would get home my Mother would scold me for being away so long. She would tell me to take a bath and when I finished with my bath, she would have a snack waiting for me. She would ask me what I had done and I would tell her of our little adventures. She would always end our conversation by warning me about rattlesnakes. I would tell her we never saw rattlesnakes and she would say, "No, but they see you. They are watching you. Just be very careful".

The nuns were still coming to Melvin every Thursday to teach catechism classes to the school children. I hated to go to the catechism classes as did most of the other children, but I was instructed by my Mother that I was to go and there was nothing else I could do but go.

The nuns continued to teach on mortal sin and venial sin. I was always very uncomfortable listening to that teaching. I knew the kind of sin I had committed with Old Grandfather was bad enough to be considered a mortal sin. Since I had not confessed my sin and I even lied to the priest, I knew I would go to hell for sure.

I became an altar boy during this time. I liked helping the priest during mass. The priest was not very kind. He would scold us badly if we made a mistake during the mass. I learned my responsibilities very well so that the priest would not scold me. I also enjoyed praying the rosary and I would pray quite often when I was by myself. I felt that if I prayed often I would be forgiven for the sins I had committed with Old Grandfather and lying to the priest.

The nuns would remind us to go to confession but I hated to do that. I knew that I could not tell the priest what

I had done with Old Grandfather, so that meant I lied every time I went to confession. That also meant that I committed a greater offense towards God. My sin kept getting bigger and bigger.

One time while I was in confession the priest asked me if I had played with my "P P". I froze. Why would he ask me that? Maybe he had found out or he just knew. After all, he was a priest. He asked me again and he sounded angry. I said no. I felt awful. I had lied to the priest again. I did not stand a chance, I was going to hell. I walked home from church wishing I was dead.

We still did not own a television set like most families did by this time. If we wanted to watch television we would go to the oldest daughter's house. Old Grandfather's oldest daughter was my Mother's comadre (best friend or close friend). Comadre's husband and my Father were good friends and they worked together frequently. Comadre's husband owned a sheep shearing machine. My Father would go with him to shear sheep and Old Grandfather was the person who picked up the wool that was sheared. I went with them once or twice but I refused to go when I saw Old Grandfather going with them.

The comadre and her husband were not rich but they always seemed to be the first Hispanic family that would buy the first of everything. For example, they were the first Hispanic family to buy a television, first family to have a telephone, their sons were the first to own a bicycle, a motorcycle, first to own a BB gun, first ones that were allowed to drive the family car, the first to buy a 1957 Chevrolet Impala hard top, etc, etc.

On Friday evenings, I would go to comadre's house and watch "I Love Lucy" and "Rin Tin Tin". Usually it would be ten o'clock at night when the last show ended. It seemed that Old Grandfather always knew when I was walking home by myself. He would wait in the dark area of the shed that was used as the laundry room and he would call out to me.

I would run home as fast as I could and open the screen door to the house making a loud noise as I ran inside and slammed the door shut behind me. My parents would get upset with me for running in the house and for slamming the door. I would pretend that I was just playing as they would repeat to me that I was not to slam the door or run in the house. I was safe. Old Grandfather had not touched me.

Because I was growing taller and was close to becoming a teenager, my Mother decided that my cot would be moved to the same room as my uncles. My Mother placed a wire towards the end of the large room that belonged to my uncle. She then placed two sheets hanging from the wire to divide the room and create a small area which would be considered my room. There, we placed my cot and an old wooden chair that was very wobbly and not safe for a person to sit on, but we used it as my bedside table. I placed an old, small blue radio at my bedside. I would fall asleep listening to the radio. I had to hold on to the ground wire sticking out from the back of the radio in order for the radio to have sound.

Every night I would go to bed, turn the radio on and hold on to the ground wire while I listened to KOMA in Oklahoma City until I would fall asleep. Once I fell asleep, I would lose my grip on the wire and the sound would go off. My uncle never complained about the radio being on when he went to bed. I guess he knew that I would fall asleep soon and the radio would go off.

The end of the school year in Melvin came, and so it was time to start getting ready to go to north Texas. As usual, my sisters and I would get excited and would talk about where each one of us would prefer we go this year. Even though my sisters knew that going to north Texas meant long hours of hard work in the fields, they were still excited about going.

After getting up very early in the morning, loading up the cars (my uncle Jose was going with us), we headed to north Texas. We ended up going to Dimmitt, Texas. We all were happy to be there in Dimmitt. We all liked that little town and we had friends there.

We moved into one of the rooms in one of the campos near the livestock yards. We never did mind where we lived. We were used to living in very poor areas in the poor sections of the towns. It was a way of life for us and we accepted it, feeling that there was no way we could change it.

My Mother would always clean the rooms where we lived very thoroughly before we would unload the car. She would sweep the ceiling, walls, and floors. She would then mop the floors with a disinfectant. My Father would go talk with the other men that lived at the campo to inquire about troqueros. The troqueros were the men that would find work and contract with the owners of the fields so that we could go work. The troqueros usually would own a big panel truck that was used to take the field workers to the fields and bring them back home to the campo. We were ready to work.

CHAPTER 10

SIXTH GRADE

As I have said before, I was tall for my age and could pass for being older than eleven years old. Because I could pass for being older than eleven years old, I was introduced to working in the fields chopping cotton.

I would have to get up at four thirty every morning to get ready for work and be at the work site to start work at six in the morning. It was still dark when the troqueros would park their trucks on the street at the entrance to the campos. Some troqueros would drive half way into the campo and park the panel truck so the field workers could climb on.

The drive to and from the fields was rough, at best, cool in the mornings and hot in the evenings. Some troqueros would place wooden benches along the panels on the trucks which would make the drive to the fields more comfortable.

If the truck did not have benches, we would have to sit on the floor of the panel truck. Sitting on the floor of the panel truck would be painful as we bounced up and down at every bump on the road or the railroad tracks. Each time the truck bounced you could see the painful expressions on the women's faces. Usually most of the men would stand rather than suffer through the painful ride home. This event took place every working day throughout the summer. I don't know that we got used to it, but I know we got used to knowing we had to take the ride.

Once we got to the fields we would grab our hoe and stand by the row of cotton plants that each person would be responsible for cutting the weeds. We would walk along the side of the row of cotton plants watching for weeds. We would walk at a normal pace but we could not lag too far behind. If we stayed behind, it would mean that we were walking too slowly and we needed to speed up. If we happened to get on a cotton row with too many weeds, the others next to you would usually help you, especially if you were a woman. When we got to the end of the row, some of which might be a mile long, we would all turn around, get another row and work our way back to the other end from where we had started. Once we got to the end, we would all drink water and repeat the same process until we had completed the entire field. Then we would go to another field and repeat the whole process.

Since this was my first year to work in the fields chopping cotton, I would walk all day along side my Father cutting all the weeds that grew in the row of cotton plants. The sun was hot and on some days, the days were calm with little or no wind blowing. I enjoyed windy days because it helped cool me off. Cloudy days were a blessing. Frequently the fields were full of Johnson grass and "quelitre" weeds which grew as tall as I was or taller.

Not once did my Father ask me how I was doing or feeling. And, not once do I remember complaining about having to work ten hours a day. It would not do any good to complain. I was just supposed to start working and not have a say about it. We were poor and I had to work, period.

Water breaks were interesting or in our present times might be thought of as "yucky". The troquero was responsible for supplying the water for the people. Most troqueros would provide ice water most of the time. The water was provided in one or two large barrels filled with water. The water glasses were usually made out of beer cans or vegetable cans with a wire tied around each end that was used as the handle for the can. No one seemed to care that we all drank water from the same water glasses and dipping the glasses into the barrels to refill with water for the next person to drink. I guess if it bothered you, you could go all day without drinking water. Good luck.

Going to the restroom out in the fields was a challenge especially for the women. There were no port-a-potties or bathrooms so women had to look for high weeds or high plants or whatever machinery that was not used or ditches. Usually the women would go in groups of three or four and took turns being look-outs for each other. Men always respected the women needing to go to the bathroom and provided privacy whenever needed and the troquero would sometimes drive the women to where they could use the bathroom if no area was available in the fields. That meant that all women would have to go at the same time and would have to wait until they were driven to the bathrooms.

At noon time, we would take thirty minutes for lunch. When we heard the troquero honk the horn of the truck, we all rushed to the truck to try and get a place that was shaded from the hot sun. If you did not find a spot that was shaded, then you would sit your thirty minutes in the hot sun to eat. I did not like sitting in the hot sun and to this day I do not like to be outside when the sun is hot.

Our lunch was always very good, but usually not enough. My Father, my two sisters and I would each have refried beans in one flour tortilla folded in half. Along with the tortilla taco, as we refer to it, we would open a can of pork and beans and all four of us shared from that one can. Sometimes we would have dessert which consisted of a small can of mixed fruit. If the troquero had soft drinks for sale, we would each buy a soft drink. If the troquero did not have drinks to sell, we would then share coffee from a thermos bottle. We all drank coffee from the same cup. We barely had time to eat our one taco and a few pork and beans then it was time to go back to the fields to work. At four-thirty, our ten hours for the day were up and we would head back home.

When we would get home, my Mother would have supper ready. Supper usually consisted of more refried beans and potatoes. Occasionally we would have some type of meat to go along with the beans and potatoes. It did not matter to me what we ate, it all tasted good to me.

When I first started working in the fields, I was getting paid thirty-five cents an hour for chopping cotton. Each one of us was getting paid that amount. That meant I made three dollars and fifty cents in a ten hour work day, which adds up to seventeen dollars and fifty cents per week. That also meant that with the four of us in my family working, we brought home seventy dollars a week.

Out of those seventy dollars, we paid ten dollars rent per week, twenty dollars per week for groceries, twenty dollars payment to the grocery store (Red & White Grocery) back home in Melvin and the rest saved for whatever necessities occurred during the week. I would get a dollar a week allowance and my sisters would get three dollars each per week for their allowance. My little sister would get fifty cents a week. My Mother used to say my little sister was very helpful at home and deserved to get an allowance. I do not remember my young sister doing much at home as far as work, ever, but she was the baby in the family and was treated as such.

Weekends were always something to look forward to. On Saturday mornings we would all take turns using the one room to bath and change. After the last member of the family had finished with his/her bath, we would all get in the car and drive twenty miles to Hereford, Texas, to do our grocery shopping as well as whatever other shopping was necessary.

My sister Emma was usually the one that always had to look for new dresses. Once the shopping was completed in late afternoon, we would head back to Dimmitt.

Once we ate supper on Saturday evenings, we would start getting ready for the Mexican dance. The Mexican dances were a must for the young and for the older people. It seemed that nearly all the Hispanic families would go to the dances. The dance was the highlight of the whole week. That was why we did not mind working hard all week. My Father liked getting to the dance early to be able to get a parking place near the dance area. Sometimes my Mother would get tired and would come and sit in the car for a short time. The dances usually started at eight in the evening and ended at one on Sunday morning. If we parked near the dance area, my Mother could enjoy listening to the music from the car.

On Sunday I would usually go to church. After church I would go to the movies and then come home. Once I got home from the movies I would help my Father start getting things ready for work next day. We did the same thing every weekend and it sounds like it would become boring, but we were actually having a great time. My sisters and I often talked about those times many years later.

We worked the whole summer chopping cotton until late August. This year we did come back to Melvin in late August before school started. Most of the chopping cotton work was done by now and soon it would be time to start picking cotton. My parents decided we would come home to Melvin instead of staying to pick cotton. Even though we would still be picking cotton in Melvin, we were tired and were ready to come home.

This was the life of Hispanic immigrants. Thousands of Hispanics from all over Texas, and even Mexico would migrate to North West Texas to work in the fields. I do not remember seeing any Anglos or African-Americans working in the fields. There probably were some working in the fields like we were, but I, myself, never saw them.

After my first summer of chopping cotton, I knew that I did not want to work the fields the rest of my life. I wanted to do a type of work that was a lot easier. This being my first year of chopping cotton, I knew I had several more years to go before I could get a job where I did not have to work in the hot sun or in the cold during the winter months. I decided then that I wanted to finish school so that I could qualify for a better job.

Even though we had come back to Melvin earlier than usual, I still had to pick cotton after school and quite often, I would miss school on Fridays to go pick cotton and help my Father out financially. Most of the Hispanic teenagers would have to pick cotton on Fridays and definitely on Saturdays.

I got to start school from the beginning of the school year. Going to school was not a problem for me. I liked school. I did not mind the homework except that I did not have anyone to help me at home. My parents did not read or write English and my older sisters had dropped out of school. I did my best. And I guess my best was good enough because I kept passing to the next grade each year. At that time, if a student did not make passing grades, that student would have to repeat that grade. I repeated the first grade once. I know of some boys and girls that had to repeat the same grade several years. I had a cousin who repeated the third grade three years. He used to say he was beginning to think that the third grade teacher was his mother.

The Thanksgiving holiday was just another day for us at home. We never had turkey for Thanksgiving. If we had enough money, my Mother would buy and fix a chicken or we would just eat beans and potatoes. That was just great for me as long as I got to go to my cousin's house to play. The cotton would all be picked by now and whatever school holiday we had off, we could play or do whatever we wanted to do.

On weekends it continued to be the usual as on weekends in north Texas. Dances on Saturday nights and church on Sundays. Actually, that was all we had to do in the little town. We did not have a theater in Melvin. If we wanted to go to the movies, we had to drive to Brady, about sixteen miles east of Melvin.

Brady is centrally located in the state of Texas and the Brady residents refer to it as the Heart of Texas. Brady, population of about six to eight thousand people, was the nearest big town where our little town families would go to the Piggly Wiggly to buy groceries and to some of the clothing stores. Brady also had a movie theater and a drive-in movie theater. It had one burger drive-in restaurant that was the hangout for teenagers.

Every time my family and I went to Brady, it would be almost an all day affair. We had an old car and my Father would drive very slowly. On a good day he would speed up to fifty miles per hour, but usually forty to forty-five miles an hour was the fastest he drove. Emma, my younger sister, and I always sat in the back seat and usually fell asleep. We were able to take a good nap going to and from Brady. It was a boring drive but for some reason, any time my parents mentioned going to Brady, we all wanted to go.

My friends were few, except for the neighbor's children who continued to be my friends. They all had bicycles except me, so I would run alongside them. If they peddled their bicycles too fast for me to keep up with them, I would just stop running and walk back home. I felt that if they did not want to wait for me, they probably did not want me along. And that was fine with me. I did not ask for a bicycle because I knew my parents did not have the money.

My older sister noticed that the boys had bicycles and I would run alongside them. She felt sorry for me and worked, mostly ironing clothes, to buy me a bicycle. She asked the neighbors to drive her to Brady and she bought me a bicycle. If I remember correctly, I think she said she paid twenty five dollars for the bicycle. It was a great surprise for me and I loved my bicycle. Now, I could ride along with my friends. It also made it easier to ride to visit with my cousins. My cousins had bicycles, but they had bought them from someone they knew.

My cousin David and I would often ride to the school building and sit in front of the auditorium. We would sit there and just talk. We would both talk about what we wished we could do when we grew up. My cousin wanted to go into the service. All of his older brothers had been in the service and he felt he wanted to do that also. My cousin liked to smoke. Sometimes we would steal one or two cigarettes from our parents and he would smoke them while we talked. I did not like the taste of cigarettes, so I would give him my cigarette.

Ever since that first evening with Old Grandfather, I began to feel that I was alone. I did not have other friends and I told myself that it was okay, I understood. After all, why should they want to be my friends? I was bad, sinful and I did not deserve to have any friends. Even though my cousin David and I were close, at least closer than any one I knew, I could not tell him about Old Grandfather. It would destroy our friendship. I did not want anyone to know about Old Grandfather. He had not touched me in a long time and so I felt maybe it would all go away. Maybe I could forget. Maybe someday, I would not remember what had happened with Old Grandfather.

But every time I saw Old Grandfather, I felt a deep fear. What if he told my parents? What if he told someone? When I was away from Old Grandfather, I would tell myself that if he ever tried to touch me again, I was bigger than he was now and I could beat him up. I felt angry enough and big enough to do it. But, once I saw him, fear would take over and I forgot about how angry I had been. Fear would take over.

As I may have mentioned before, Old Grandfather walked everywhere he went. He did not have a car and he may not have ever learned to drive, so he walked. If I happened to see him walking towards me on the same street I was walking on, I would turn around and walk around to a different street that would take me several blocks out of my way, just as long as I did not have to meet him face to face. I would even look back to see if he was following me, to make sure he was not right behind me. Occasionally, I would be at his daughter's house watching television and he would come in and see me and smile. He would make a kidding remark about how he saw me the other day and he waved and I did not wave back. Or how he saw me the other night as I was walking home and he asked me a question and I did not answer him.

Then his daughter or wife would look at me and tell me that I should always be nice to my elders. They mentioned that they would have to tell my Mother that I was being disrespectful. I would get up and go home so afraid that Old Grandfather would tell my parents what happened. Or he might even tell his wife and daughter and I would be punished for what happened. I would go home and when it was time to go to bed, I would pray very hard that Old Grandfather would not tell anyone.

The school year ended soon enough and then it was time for us to head up to north Texas to work. We were not sure where we would be going but we packed our car and headed north. We ended up going to Dimmitt and found a different "campo" in town. The campo had several families that were there for the summer to work the fields.

Most of the families that lived in the same campo worked the same fields. We would all hook-up with the same troquero and rode the same panel truck to and from work. Again, I did not mind riding in the large panel trucks along with the other people but I hated that my older sister had to struggle to climb onto the panel truck. But she had to work and there was nothing I could do about it.

My family and I enjoyed living in Dimmitt. I worked hard and enjoyed going shopping on Saturdays and going to the dance on Saturday night. I also went to the movies on Sunday afternoon. Most of the Hispanic teens and even those up in their 20's and early 30's would go to the movies. Boys and girls would meet there for a date or just sit watching the movie. After the movie I would go home and start getting ready for work next day.

Occasionally my Father would take us to the dance on Sunday nights. He would set rules though. Get up early without having to be awakened several times. So on Monday morning, my sisters and I would immediately wake up on my Father's first "wake-up" call. I would quickly get out of bed because if I lay there a few minutes, it would be much harder for me to get out of bed.

The dances would end at twelve midnight and we would get up at four-thirty in the morning. We would not get much sleep by the time we got home from the dance and went to bed. But we were young and wanted to have fun, and going to the dances was fun for us. I loved to dance, but I did not dance because I was way too shy to ask a girl to dance. I felt I was ugly and the girls would turn me down. But I went anyway and watched the others dance.

The summer went by fast and my parents started planning as to when we would go back home. We would all be excited about going back home because, even though we liked living in Dimmitt, the work was hard and by the end of summer we were tired and ready for a few days of rest before cotton season began.

The drive back to Melvin was long and tiring, but we got to sleep most of the way home. We made very few stops along the way and my father drove fifty miles per hour most of the way home. We would always make it home safely and early enough that we would get to unload the car. My Mother would fix supper in her kitchen. Right away it felt like home again. We would all sleep very soundly that night and wake up fresh and just plain happy to be home again.

CHAPTER 11

SEVENTH GRADE

Shortly after we got back from Dimmitt, I visited my cousins. We would spend as much time together as we could before school started. I would ride my bicycle to their house and spend most of the day with them. If I did not go to their house, I would stay home and spend most of the day by myself. The neighbors' boys and I did not spend too much time together anymore. Our friendships were not as they used to be.

My cousin David and I spent a lot of time in the woods and we talked a lot. We did a lot of daydreaming. There were so many things that we wanted to do, but not really believing we could do them. We visited each other and went walking through the pastures and walked along the railroad tracks, just doing nothing.

The times that I was by myself, I would think about my future, what I wanted to do. I really had no idea as to what I wanted to do, but I knew I wanted to do something besides working in the fields and picking cotton. I felt that by now, maybe I should already know what I wanted to do after I graduated from high school. But I didn't know.

I started the seventh grade and tried to do well in school. I made passing grades and that was important to me. I taught myself to read and write Spanish during this school year. I used newspapers written in Spanish to read and practice writing. I played basketball but was not really good at it and usually did not play during the games.

The rest of the school year went by quickly and very soon we were planning on going back to north Texas again. Again we would get all excited about going to north Texas and this time my Father told us we would be going back to Dimmit. We knew that it would be hard work, but like I have said before, we liked going to Dimmit.

Once we arrived in Dimmit, my Father found a different "campo" from last year. All the "campos" were in a very run down part of the town. There were dirt roads and when it rained, the streets were muddy and slippery. Drivers had to be very careful driving on the muddy roads or they would slide into the ditches. When it was dry, there was lots of dust, especially when cars would drive by or if it was windy. The compo was near a livestock pen area. Cattle and pigs would be penned there. When the wind was from the direction of the livestock pen area, the odor was awful. Flies were aplenty. The restrooms were outdoor restrooms and that also contributed to the odors and flies.

The rooms that were rented out to the families were small one room quarters. My Mother would immediately clean the room that we would be living in. She would dust, sweep, mop and spray. The room would be very clean before we would bring in our belongings. My Mother would decide which side of the room would be considered the kitchen. We had a two-burner gas stove that sat on four prong-like legs. The army cot that we always brought along would be spread out and the small mattress and blankets and quilts would be placed on the cot. The screens on the two small windows would be repaired to keep out the flies and mosquitoes. My Father would go out and look for a troquero who would use us out in the fields. There were many troqueros, so finding and hooking up with one was easy.

We soon started working out in the fields. My Father, my two older sisters and I would work ten hours a day five or six days a week. My Mother and my young sister would stay home. When we got home in the evenings, my Mother would have supper ready for us to eat. We had five gallon cans and crates that we used to sit on. We would eat with the plate of food on our laps or would set the plate on the cot, using the cot as a table. After we got through eating we would sit outside by the building and rest until it was time to go to bed.

Bath times were three times a week. The person taking a bath would have to heat up some water, set up the round wash tub, and close the door to the room. The rest of the family would sit outside until the family member was through bathing. The family member was responsible for throwing out the bath water and cleaning up the room. It was a big job setting up for taking a bath and cleaning up afterwards, but we did it without fussing.

On weekends we would drive to Hereford, Texas, which was about twenty miles from Dimmit. Hereford was larger than Dimmitt and therefore had more stores for shopping. When we would get to Hereford, the first thing we would do is eat. If we all wanted hamburgers, we would eat at a small burger place that sold seven hamburgers for a dollar. The hamburgers were big burgers with everything included. Fries were sold separately. I have no idea how that place made money, but we were very glad that we could buy the burgers at that price.

At other times my parents would want to eat in a restaurant, so we would all go to a Mexican restaurant and eat there. We did not eat in any restaurants managed by white people or frequented by white people because usually we were not treated nice. The white people were not very kind and so we mostly stayed on our side of town or ate in Mexican restaurants that were located in the areas where we lived.

The movie theater in Dimmit allowed Hispanics but we had to sit on one side of the theater. There was an usher that would walk up and down the aisle with a flashlight making sure that the Hispanics stayed on their side of the theater. If a Hispanic was caught sitting on the wrong side of the theater, they would be escorted out. No one that I know of ever protested. It was the Hispanics way of life.

Then, there were the Spanish dances every Friday, Saturday, and Sunday nights. We went to the Saturday night dances for sure, but Fridays and Sundays depended on how my parents felt. Usually we did not go on those days. One of my sisters would get very upset if we did not go, but she would have to just get over it. It was back to work on Monday.

Soon it was time for us to come back to Melvin. We would pack the car the night before, wake up at five in the morning and be on the road by six. My Father was a morning person and expected the rest of us to be the same. But on the mornings when we would be driving back to Melvin, we would eagerly get up without having to be called more than once.

Our drive home would be as usual, long, hot and tiring. But once we got to where we could see the Melvin water tower, we would start looking for our shoes and getting ready to get off the car. We were home again.

CHAPTER 12

EIGHTH GRADE

Eighth grade was a good year as far as school goes. I did the best I could to make good grades. I had difficulty, but I kept on trying. I did my homework without any assistance. Somehow I was able to make good grades. My eighth grade teacher was not an easy teacher to learn from. He just sat behind his desk and talked in a monotone voice during the whole class. It was boring and hard to know when to take notes. His tests were from what he talked about in class. I was very lucky that I passed at the end of the school year. Other teachers would take the time to explain the material if we did not understand. But this man never took the time to explain things. If questions were asked, he looked at you and continued talking.

This year I became friends with another boy in school; his name was also David. We were close friends all through high school until he graduated. He was a class ahead of me in school but we were able to spend a lot of time together because we had study hall and physical education (PE) together.

David and I spent a lot of time at the school gym playing basketball after school and on weekends. We both became good at playing half court basketball and we often had other boys or men challenge us. I was slim and my friend was overweight, but we had practiced together for so long that we were able to outplay almost anybody that challenged us. We had fun going through high school together.

My sisters and I were teenagers and still living in a one room barrack. My sisters did not have any privacy and every time they had to change clothes, they had to let my uncle know that they would be in his room changing clothes. We never complained about the fact that we were teenagers and still lived in the one large room.

One day I heard my Mother telling my Father that we needed to look for another place to live so that the girls could have some privacy. My Mother also said she did not like the fact that my uncle would come into our room during cold weather and sit in front of the open flame space heater and stay there nearly all day long. During cold weather, there was not that much work, so both my Father and my uncle would be home all day.

My Father told my Mother that we could not afford to get a house because he did not have a job or money. He ended the conversation by telling my Mother that getting a house was out of the question. My Mother responded that there would be some way that we could get a house. She ended with "Donde hay querer, hay poder," (where there is a will, there is a way).

I have no idea how my Mother came up with the idea of getting the specific house that we got. I do know that my Mother had called the owner of the house who lived in San Antonio, Texas, and talked to her about the house. The house was right off a curve on the paved road that lead to Brady via what people referred to as the back way.

The house was an old house that had been vacant for many years. It was sitting on an acre of land and also had an old army barrack in the same lot a few feet from the house. There were tall weeds all around the house almost taller than we were. The owner had told my Mother that, years ago, some people had rented the house but did not stay long claiming that the house was haunted. The owner told my Mother what the renters had heard and had caused them to move out.

I remember that my three sisters, my Mother and I got in the car and drove over to the old house. We had taken a garden hoe and made a walking trail from the front gate to the front porch. My Mother in the lead walked to the front porch and we all followed. The porch was old with some broken boards and it looked like it might fall any minute. The front door was unlocked and we all entered the house. The house looked big inside, all empty rooms and clean. We walked behind my Mother who walked slowly looking at the walls and windows as we walked into the small dining room. The dining room was on a corner of the house and there were windows on the two sides that were the outer walls. Then we walked into the next room which was the kitchen. The kitchen had one small counter top with a cabinet underneath and with a large kitchen sink. There was a water faucet over the sink that indicated there would be running water inside.

We continued following my Mother to the next room which was a small room which may have been a bathroom or could be made into a bathroom. We followed my Mother to the next room which was a large room with two small closets. Straight ahead we walked into the last room which was also a big room with no closets only three large windows and a door that opened to the front porch. When we had walked all through the house walking behind my Mother, she stopped and turned to go through the house one more time walking back the same way we had come through but this time she looked at the house a little more closely.

When we came to the front room where we had entered the house, my Mother again turned around facing us and asked us what we thought. And we did tell her what we thought. We thought it was a castle. We all thought it was the most beautiful house in the whole world. It had separate bedrooms. How wonderful. We all became very excited and walked back to the two large bedrooms. The girls decided that the end room that had the door opening to the front porch would be their room. The middle room with the two small closets would be my room. I thought it was a wonderful room.

We were all talking excitedly until my Mother told us to listen closely. She then told us that the owner had told her the house was haunted and asked what we thought about it. My older sister said she did not believe in ghosts and we all agreed. We would share with the ghosts. We all wanted the house. The house would need lots of repair work. As long as it had been by itself with no one living here, all the windows were intact, not one window was broken or cracked. We all then went separate ways exploring and my sisters talking about where they would place furniture, etc.

That night my Mother waited until my uncle had gone to his room before she mentioned to my Father about the house. We did not want to be nosy but we were all very quiet. She told him we had gone to see the house, that the children liked it and that we should get the house. As we all had expected, my Father said no because we did not have any money to pay for the house. My Mother explained to him that the owner of the house was behind on her taxes but if we bought the house, she would pay the back taxes.

She again, went on to explain to my Father that the children were all grown and that we needed separate rooms. She told my Father that the girls had no privacy and that we would get the house somehow. My Father mumbled a few words and walked out the door. When my Father would get angry, which was rare, he would say a few bad words and leave the house. He usually would go downtown to the pool hall and visit with the rest of the men.

But this time my Mother meant business. She did not give up or give in. She stood her ground. The owner of the house had told my Mother that the house would cost two thousand dollars, which included the Army barrack on the same lot and an acre land. She had also told my Mother that we could pay it as we were able. My Mother told my dad that we would move and if he wanted to stay here with his brother, that it was fine with her, but that her children needed rooms for privacy and that she would get the house. My Father noticed how serious she was so he started asking specific questions about the house, cost, payments, etc. When we heard him asking the questions, we knew that we would be getting the house. We all then started talking excitedly about the beautiful house.

My parents rarely argued in front of their children. I do not remember my parents arguing. They would talk and sometimes disagree on some things but never got into an argument. They showed a lot of respect for each other. A lot of times my Father would not do things he wanted to do because he would state that my Mother would not like it. My Father used a lot of bad words but my Mother would always say that we were not allowed to say those words and we rarely use them, still. My sisters and I grew up not using those words.

I had difficulty going to sleep that night. I thought about the house and how I would have my own room. Since my Mother had told me that the middle room with the two small closets would be my room, I went to sleep thinking about that room.

The night went by fast and I was awakened by my uncle as he closed the door going to the next room to eat breakfast. I got up and got ready to go to school. I went into the next room to eat breakfast. Everyone was silent. No one was talking. I wondered if maybe something was said after I went to bed. I must have missed something. As I walked to school, I kept thinking that there was something wrong. Something happened. There was little talk. I thought we should all be very excited and happy just like we were yesterday and last night. Something must have happened. Maybe my parents found out about Old Grandfather. Or maybe Old Grandfather told my parents.

Old Grandfather still frightened me something terrible. Every time I saw him, he would give me a weird smile. He still tried to talk to me. He still wanted me to meet him. He would ask me to meet him in the ally. Sometimes he wanted me to meet him at the school building. I would just run or hurry home as fast as I could. One time I was riding my bicycle from my friend's house when I saw him walking on the side walk. I saw him about a block and a half away. I thought about turning around and finding a different route to get home. Since I was on my bicycle, I thought I would just go past him as fast as I could and not even look at him.

But Old Grandfather just started walking to get in front of my bicycle. He kept calling to me, saying he would tell my Father if I did not stop. I made it past him but I could hear him calling me. I kept on going and did not look back until I got home. I was about fifteen years old. I was afraid of him. I did not know what to think. I hated myself for being afraid of him. I hated myself for allowing him to ever touch me. I hated myself because he would tell my parents and now we would not get the house. My parents would know about the terrible thing I had done and they would hate me. They would all hate me. They barely spoke to me this morning. My sisters hated me because now they would not have their own room and have the privacy they had talked about when we were looking at the house. It was all my fault.

I always came home for lunch since school was only a block away from home. I did not know whether to go home or not. I would ask my Mother to forgive me. I would tell Old Grandfather that I was sorry that I was mean to him. When I entered the barrack, I called out to my Mother so that she would know I was home for lunch. There were beans on the stove and tortillas on the table. My Mother was not home and I was relieved. But I kept wondering why no one was home. We all usually ate together or at least I never ate by myself. I ate and went back to school.

At school I was able to forget about the house and Old Grandfather and was able to concentrate on my studies. Our last class was physical education and so playing was good for me. I did not have time to think about anything other than the game we were playing. On the way home from school, I noticed that our car was home. I ran home to see where my Mother had gone and why she had not been home at noon.

When I entered the barrack, my older sister was waiting for my younger sister and me. We had to hurry up and change clothes because we needed to come and help. I asked as to where we needed to go help and my older sister said, "At the house. We need to cut the weeds." My younger sister and I quickly changed clothes and I did not even care that there had not been a snack for me. I just wanted to get to the "new" house. We worked at the new house until dark. Then we all went home tired but all excited about the new home. I am not sure exactly when the deal was made, who was present when the deal was made. All I know is that I was very excited about the new house and now I would have my own room.

Again I went to bed very excited. I was excited because of the new house, but also because now I knew why my Mother had not been home at noon when I came for lunch. Even though I did not know why everyone seemed to be very quiet this morning, I knew that they were not angry at me. Old Grandfather had not told my parents. I prayed that he would not tell my parents about me being bad. If only he would not say anything before we moved. Once we moved, I would be away from him and he would not be trying to touch me. I fell asleep.

I told my friend David what we had being doing at the new house. My friend did not have his own bed room either, so he was happy for me.

I kept thinking of the way I would decorate my room. I would bring my cot and place it by the window. I had a window all to myself. The room would look big with just a cot for a bed, but I did not care about that. I was just extremely happy to have my own room. I could tell my sisters felt the same way. They kept talking about the way they would decorate their room as they cleaned their room and the whole inside of the house. My Mother had told me to cut weeds in front of the house so that we would have paths to carry the furniture and things into the house. I did not mind doing that because I knew once we got rid of the weeds we would keep the yard looking nice.

The whole family was excited. My Father never showed much emotion on anything, but I just assumed he was excited. I could tell that my Mother was very happy. She tried to hide it by being the supervisor while we cleaned the house and cleared the front yard. She was such a hard worker and never complained about the work. She just did the work because it had to be done, as she would say.

My Father had asked my Mother about moving the furniture. He had commented that he did not know how it would be done, since we did not have a truck to use to move the furniture. My Mother told my Father that she would get everything moved except the big heavy objects like the refrigerator, stove, dining table, wringer washer and sofa. He would have to find a way to move those items.

We had lived with my uncle all these years, but he decided to stay in the Army barrack. My Father had told him he could live in the other Army barrack next to the house, but he said he wanted to stay.

So moving day was here. My Mother had talked to some of her comadres and the comadres came with their cars to help move. We would load up the cars and then drive over to the house which was about eight blocks from where we lived. I would ride my bicycle to the house and help unload the cars. By mid afternoon we had moved everything except those big, heavy items that my Father would have to move. It had been fairly easy moving all those boxes, mattresses, bed frames, one large round top trunk, and clothing in cars.

My Father had gone to work so he was very surprised when he came home and saw all that had been moved in cars. My Father used a pick-up truck that belonged to the older daughter of Old Grandfather. Since my Father worked for the older daughter's husband, the husband also helped move the large heavy items. I had to help, but again, I did not mind at all. It meant getting away from Old Grandfather and I would help in any way I could to get away from him.

On Saturday night, we spent our first night in the new house. Mind you, it was an old, old house, but to us it was new and we did not see the old in the house. To us, it was a beautiful house. My Mother had gotten a bed from some-where and I slept in a regular sized bed that was all mine. At night my sisters closed the door that opened into my room and I closed the other two doors that opened into the kitchen, and the third door into my parent's bed room. I slept soundly in my own room.

Very soon we got all settled in and now it was time to explore our new property. My Mother and I had already gotten all the weeds cut in the front of the house and piled them up in the back yard. Now we had started clearing up the yard towards the back of the house. There were some posts set up for a clothesline but there was no wire for the line. We took the wire from the clothesline that we had in the other place and set up a new clothesline at the new place. We all had a great time getting the place looking like a home.

I spent a lot of time cleaning the barrack and wondering what we could use the place for. I did not have to wonder for long because my father told us that his brother wanted to sell the other barrack and move into this one. The large room closest to the house would be his room.

We all worked hard to clean up the house and the yard but we were all very happy. We had never lived in a house where we had running water inside. We would only have cold water but we did not care because it was inside the house. That was a great luxury for us. The whole time we worked cleaning up the property, we never thought about the house being haunted.

Winter was here and it was our first winter in the new house. The winter was cold and so was the house. The first snow storm we had, I woke up in the morning and got dressed and went into the kitchen. My Father asked me if I had seen the snow. I looked out the window and the ground was covered with snow. It was beautiful. I wanted to get my sisters to see the snow but they were still in bed. My Mother told me to go wake them up.

When I opened the door and walked into their room, it was freezing. I called out to them and they mumbled something about being cold. I looked around the room and started laughing. There was snow on the floor in the room. And it was not melted, either. They looked at the snow and they too, started to laugh. My parents came to look and soon we were all laughing. The snow had blown in through the cracks around the window frames. But we still loved the house.

It seemed like such a short time but now it was time to go to north Texas and work. We still got excited to go to Dimmitt, Texas. We had gotten to know people there and it felt like a second hometown. Working in the fields, ten hours a day was hard work. Days were hot and we could not really wish for rain because if it rained, we did not work. But the cloudy days were a great blessing. We still went to the dances every Saturday night and on special occasions, on Sunday nights.

We worked through the hot summer as usual, ten hours a day, five days a week. The days were hot out in the middle of the fields with no shade from the hot sun. Most of the time there was no wind and tall weeds that were hard to cut. The only relief we got from the heat was the ice cold water we would drank when we got to the end of the rows of cotton plants. When we picked cotton in the fall, we would have some cool or cold mornings. We would get warmed up once we started picking the cotton.

I began to hate to have to work in the fields. I wanted to work in a place that was cool in the summer and warm in the winter. I wanted to have a job where I did not have to work so hard and work such long hours. I wanted to finish school and work at a bank where I could be comfortable while working and make good money. I do not know where I got the idea that I would make good money working at the bank. But that is what I felt I wanted to do.

Soon it was time to come back to Melvin so that I could start school at the beginning of the school year. Again we became excited about coming back home to Melvin. Now we had a house to go home to and I had my own bedroom. We all got up early in the morning, loaded up our car and we headed home.

CHAPTER 13

NINTH GRADE

We arrived in Melvin late afternoon. We drove into the dirt drive way and hurriedly got out of the car and rushed inside. We all went about the house looking to see what changes had occurred while we were gone. Things inside the house were dusty but everything seemed to be as we had left it.

It felt so good to be home. My bed was still the way I had left it. Everything inside our home seemed to be just the way we had left it. My uncle had stayed here, but he stayed in the barrack. He only came into the house when he had to eat. The weeds had grown tall again. My uncle had not kept up the front yard. As usual, he never did anything to help us, that included clearing up the yard. My Father did not help either. They would sit on the front porch and talk, watch cars drive by and they would argue. They would argue about the most insignificant things. Never the less, I was very happy to be home.

The next few days would be spent cleaning, dusting, washing and rearranging. My Mother would always clean the entire house after a long absence. My Mother kept a clean house. She worked hard to make the old house look nice. And the old house did look different. The front porch still looked like it may fall any minute, but the whole house and yard had that feeling of warmth, of home.

Our old house was so comfortable and warm. Not warmth from heat, but a different kind. Like the warmth you feel when your mother places her arms around you and holds you tight because she is so happy to see you after being gone for awhile. The house gave me that warm feeling, protected and safe. We never thought about the possibility of the house being haunted. We loved the old house. When we were asked about the house being haunted, we would just say that we loved the old house and if it was haunted, we did not mind sharing. Eventually, people stopped asking if the house was haunted or if we had seen anything or heard strange noises.

High school was different for me. I had to study harder to be able to make the lowest passing grade. Math was my worst enemy. I tried so hard to learn and know algebra, but I was not able to understand it. Algebra was taught by the school coach. He may have known what he was talking about, but it did not make sense to me. I never asked any questions in class, so that made it harder for me to learn. I always felt that what I had to ask was dumb and every one would laugh at my dumb questions. So I kept quiet.

My friend David, who was one class ahead of me, and I continued being good friends. We went to the ball games together. I had to sneak in through the back fence because I did not have the money to pay to go in to watch the football game. Before I got into high school, my parents, my youngest sister and I would drive and park outside the fence and watch from the car. We could not see the game but we could see the score board and hear the loud speaker as the announcer called the game, play by play. It was fun that way also. My friend had money to get in to see the games and to buy refreshments if he wanted to. But can you imagine, I did not have twenty five cents to pay to get in to watch the football game. I attended nearly all the football games and basketball games anyway.

My cousin David, who was in my class, and I were still close, but he started to be distant. Not because he did not want to talk to me but because he started thinking about going into the service or dropping out of school. I wanted to continue going to school. As I had said before, I hated working in the fields. My thinking that I would work in a bank helped me to stay in school. I never told anybody about my thoughts because I knew they would laugh at me. I would laugh to myself and think, can you imagine if I was working in a bank.

Old Grandfather was not around anymore to where I could see him. I did not have to see him try to get my attention by coughing loudly whenever he saw me or, by grabbing his crouch if I saw him, or if people were around he would smile at me and ask me how I was doing, acting like we were good friends. I just knew that everyone could tell what I had done. Everyone would know how terrible I had been. I felt I had done something horribly wrong. Every time I saw Old Grandfather I would feel so dirty, so bad. I would feel as if I was no good, that I was not worthy of anyone liking me, much less loving me. I would ask God to forgive me, but never felt that God forgave me for such a terrible act as what I had done. I would always pray to try to forget or let myself think I had been forgiven.

Being Catholic did not help. The nuns had made me feel that I would go to hell if I sinned. What I did was not a venial sin. I had committed a mortal sin. I was going to hell. I had no one to talk to. And boy, did I pray. I would go to sleep praying. I just did not want to go to hell. I did not want to burn in the fires of hell forever, as the nuns would tell us. I wanted to be good. I wanted to be someone that my parents could be proud of. I thought that if I became a priest, maybe then I would be forgiven. God would forgive me then.

I had been an altar boy until the priest told me to find some younger boys and train them as altar boys. I had enjoyed being an altar boy and thought that maybe I would want to become a priest. I told my Mother that I wanted to become a priest. My Mother did not even look at me when she responded by saying, "No. I don't want you to become a priest. If you become a priest, the church will send you away and I will never get to see you. I love you and I want you here with us." I was stunned when she said that. My Mother loved the Lord, prayed, went to church, and always made us give God thanks for the food we had just got through eating. I thought she would be very happy to hear me say I wanted to be priest. I was very happy to hear her say she loved me, but then I thought, if she only knew the person that I really was. So now I would have to find another way to save myself from going to hell.

But I was happy. I loved our new home and I loved my room. I also enjoyed spending time in the Army barrack. My uncle lived in the large room closest to the house and I spent time in the room farthest from the house. There was a small room between the two large rooms that was used for storage. I even thought of asking my parents if I could move to the large room but I never did ask. I felt that they would not want me to move into that room.

The school year went by fast and then it was time to go back to Dimmitt, Texas. We again got all excited about going. We did not think about the hard work awaiting us. We did not think about that until we were in the middle of the fields, under the hot sun, wishing it would rain, or whatever else, except being there.

But we got to Dimmitt and found a small one room cubicle that we called our apartment. This was the smallest room so far that we had ever lived in and the six of us lived there.

We worked during the week, went to Hereford, Texas, on Saturdays, on Saturday nights we went to the dance and Sunday afternoons, we went to the movies.

This summer, sometime in August, Emma eloped with a man that we all had known for a long time. My Mother was very upset, to say the least. We were worried because we did not know that she had run off. She just did not come back from the movies or where ever she had asked permission to go.

My Mother did not sleep all night and cried a lot. I have no idea how my parents found out where my sister had gone. My sister had run off to Levelland, Texas. We loaded up the car and here we went to Levelland, Texas which was maybe about one hundred fifty miles from Dimmitt. My Father's sister also lived in Levelland, so we went to work in Levelland until it was time to come back to Melvin. We all hated to leave my sister in Levelland, but she was married now. My Mother cried when we left, but we made it to Melvin and we all seemed to be happy to be home.

CHAPTER 14

TENTH TO TWELFTH GRADES

I started school and continued my friendship with David, who was one class ahead of me. We played basketball in the gym on weekends, that is, after all the cotton had been picked. There was nothing for teenagers to do in Melvin. If we wanted to go to the movies, we had to go to Brady. And we did go on occasion. But mostly, we stayed in Melvin and David and I played basketball.

My younger sister had a best friend, Margie, who was in her same class in school. My Mother told me that Margie was a very good girl and that I should become interested in her. And so I started dating the girl who eventually became my wife.

My cousin dropped out of school after ninth grade. There were twelve of us left in my class. I enjoy telling people I graduated eleventh in my class. They are impressed until I tell them there were only twelve students in my class. I was the only Hispanic boy in the class and there were two Hispanic girls. I still enjoyed going to school but Algebra and Plane Geometry were hard. Math was like a nightmare for me. I hated it because I did not understand it. I enjoyed English and enjoyed writing essays. My English teacher was very nice. She made English interesting.

On November 23, 1963 President John F. Kennedy was shot in Dallas, Texas. I was in my History class when our teacher informed us. Our teacher lived next to the school building and he took our class to his house to watch the news on television. I remember we all sat very quietly listening to what was being shown on television related to the shooting of our President. We went back to the school building at the end of our class period. I remember we all walked back to the class room very quietly no one saying a word.

Margie and I dated all through the tenth to twelfth grade. At the time we were dating, I really felt I loved her. She was pretty, very nice and comfortable to be around. We went to the school events and enjoyed being together. But while I enjoyed being with her, there was something within me that I did not know how to deal with or think about.

I found some men very attractive. I tried to squelch the feelings by changing my thoughts, forcing myself to get busy doing something so I would not think like that. Old Grandfather was still alive but I no longer saw him. That was such a relief for me. I still thought of the awful things I had done and still felt it had been my fault. But now I had these other feelings and I did not know what to do. I prayed.

My younger sister was fifteen years old now and it seemed that everywhere I went, she had to go with me.

I'm sure you have heard of "Mary had a little lamb". I did not mind it for most of the time but then she started dating an older man, at least six years older. He came from a large family that we had been friends with and very often had been at the same places when we had gone up north to Dimmitt. You see, everybody knew everybody in Melvin.

My Father hated the thought of my young sister dating this older man, but my sister did not listen. The usual thing we did was that my sister would go with me when I went to see Margie. Vincent, my sister's boyfriend, would be there or come by and my sister would get in his car and they would drive off. They would be back a few minutes before nine pm, which was the time that I was supposed to leave Margie's house.

One night, my sister and Vincent did not come back. I waited as long as I could and then Margie told me that she felt that my sister would not come back tonight. They had eloped. I went home hating to tell my parents. My parents had already gone to bed when I got home. The house was dark as I walked into their bedroom. When they heard me walk inside the house, my Father yelled at me for being so late.

I called out to my Mother and told her that my sister had run off with Vincent. My mother started to cry. My Father started cussing. My Mother got up and sat in a chair in their room. All this went on with the lights out. I did not dare turn any lights on. I did not want to be in the same room with them. I turned and went into my room.

Earlier that evening, my older sister had told my Father that she was going to the movies with Vincent's sister and brother. My Father had told my older sister that she could not go. Imagine that. My sister was close to thirty years old and my Father did not want her to go to the movies with friends. My older sister went anyway. When I heard the car that was bringing my older sister from the movies, I walked to the door between my room and my sisters' room. My older sister, not knowing that my younger sister had run off, started knocking on the side window of her room trying to wake my younger sister to let her into their room. Their room had a door that opened onto the porch.

The house was still all dark, but all of us were awake. My Mother was sitting in the girls room, crying. No one moved when my older sister kept knocking on the window. Finally my older sister walked over to the porch and I unlocked the door. Because the house was all dark, my older sister thought my parents were asleep and did not see my Mother sitting on the chair. My older sister whispered something to me. Then my Mother yelled loudly in an angry voice saying, "See? See what happens when you all do not mind your Father?" It scared my sister and she screamed. I laughed. My Father cussed. My Mother yelled at me to go to bed. I ran to my room and closed the door. I went to bed and went to sleep, but not until I had a good laugh.

So that left only my older sister and me at home. My older sister sometimes went to work doing babysitting jobs out of town. She worked with ladies that had grown up in Melvin but were now married and with their own children. They would come and take my sister as their live-in baby sitter. That would leave only me at home. It was nice not having my sisters there. But it was okay having them there also.

I continued going to school. I was determined to graduate from school and work at the bank. But I also continued to work in the fields during summer and to pick cotton during cotton season. After my junior year in high school, my parents and I went to Dimmitt to work in the fields.

This year my Mother also worked in the fields with my Father and me. My Mother had not worked full time in the fields chopping cotton before, but this year she did work full time. Since it was only the three of us, she said she did not want to stay home by herself. My Father was not too sure she should work, but once my Mother made up her mind to do something, that was it. She did look cute in her work clothes. She was only four feet eleven inches tall and plump, okay, overweight, alright, considered obese by some standards. She wore a dress over her blue jeans, a long sleeve shirt over her dress, tennis shoes, and a bonnet or sometimes a straw sombrero. But she was a working woman and she never complained.

When I started working in the fields at age eleven, we were getting paid thirty five cents an hour. Now we were working for a dollar an hour. We thought we were making big bucks. We had never gotten paid a dollar an hour before. We were able to save more money this time to take back to Melvin.

But I still had only two pairs of blue jeans and three shirts. That did not change. And only one pair of shoes. I remember my Father saying a few bad words because the blue jeans had gone up in price, from $3.25 to $3.75. He thought it was very expensive. My shoes usually cost ten to fifteen dollars. During my junior school year, I had missed a few days of school because I did not have shoes to wear. My shoes had big holes in the soles. My Mother had cut out card board in-soles but the card board did not hold out at all. I would be dragging pieces of card board after wearing them for a short while.

I got my high school ring in the eleventh grade. The ring cost twenty five dollars. My Mother and I saved all the small change we could get, every penny, nickel and dime we could get. When the ring came in, I took the coffee can to the bank and the teller at the bank and I counted all the change. There were a few dollar bills, but not many. Just writing this makes me think, damn, we were poor.

Margie and I got engaged during my junior year in high school. I bought her an engagement ring with a very, very small diamond. That was all I could afford.

My senior year went by rather fast. I played sports and spent much of the time practicing. I still picked cotton during my senior year. Even though I was the only one left at home with my parents, I still had to work in the fields. Two of my sisters had married and my older sister was in Fort Worth working.

My parents did not place restrictions as to what time I should be home at night. I pretty much went where I wanted to go, whenever I wanted. I never abused my liberty to come and go as I pleased. There were many times that I wished my parents would have said no to my going out. My parents were very good to me. But I felt alone, lonely and I always felt I did not deserve to be loved. I had been bad and I felt I was just completely a lost cause.

I was happy but for some reason, I would get feelings of loneliness. I felt worthless, felt like as if I was not deserving of anything good that happened to me. I did not know why I would get those feelings. I felt everyone else was better than I was. I tried to make myself feel otherwise, but it never helped. The feelings would finally go away and I would be okay for awhile.

I played basketball during my senior year in high school. During a basketball game that we played against Lohn, I scored the winning points at the very last few seconds. We won the game. It was a great big deal for us, since we had not won any games that year. My parents never attended any of my games. I sometimes wish they had attended at least a few games.

During my Junior-Senior play, I had a major part in the play. I remember that during practice about two days before the play, my teacher took me aside and asked me if I could act my character role as she would show me. Earlier that evening, she had sat all of us down and told us that we were doing really badly and that she felt if we were not serious about the play, we needed to refund the money on tickets we had already sold. When she asked me if I could do the acting if she showed me how, I said yes.

I still remember the name of my character as Luis Catarro, an Italian. And my very first line was, " Aha, your joosta the girl I coma too see." Can you believe that, at my age and after so many years, I can still remember that line from the play? I remember that I did my part just as my teacher had instructed me. If I do say so myself, I did very good. I was given many compliments for my performance. But my Father was not there. He did not get to see that I was able to do some things well. My Mother was there and she was happy for me. At the time, my Father not being there did not bother me. I was used to him not attending any of the school functions or events that any of us, his children, had been involved in.

One of the most favorite persons in my high school life was my English teacher. She treated me and talked to me as if she believed in me. During my senior year, she gave me one of her school pictures. On the back of the picture she wrote, "To Joe, who will succeed in life". I read that line so many times for many years after. If I felt lost, which was quite often, I would read that line. If times got really tough, which also were quite often, I would read that line. It helped me get through so many hardships when I felt like giving up, as you will read later on.

The custom in the school was for seniors to take their final exams and be out one week early at the end of the school year. I passed all my exams. I was through with high school. I was excited but somewhat lost. I did not know what I was going to do. I wanted to go to business school but my Father had told me flat out that he had no money. I was disappointed, to say the least. What was I going to do?

Graduation night was fun and at the same time weird for me. It seemed like finality. It was exciting but scary because I kept thinking, now what?

My senior year seemed to have gone by quickly. I was feeling I needed to decide what all I would be doing after graduation. I was nineteen years old when I graduated due to my having to repeat the first grade. Even though, I had been engaged to Margie all this time, I had not thought about marriage. After my graduation Margie left with her family to go to Kansas to work in the fields for the summer. My parents and I went to Levelland to work in the fields.

From Levelland I went to Abilene, Texas, to go to business school. I still wanted to work at a bank where all the money was and decided that going to business school would help. So I started business school. Business school was not hard. But I did find out I hated to work with numbers. Math was the one thing I was not good at in school and now I had to deal with numbers. After business school, I went back to Levelland with my parents.

CHAPTER 15

MARRIAGE

After I had been out of business school for a short time, I received a letter from Uncle Sam. I was being instructed to go for my physical to go into the Army. That changed everything. I wrote to Margie and informed her of the letter and asked her if she would marry me. She said she would.

My younger sister, her husband and I went to Kansas and Margie came back with me. Her grandfather was not too happy with the idea of Margie marrying me, but she came back with me. Margie's father lived in Abernathy, near Lubbock, which was near Levelland and he was the one that signed for Margie to marry me, since she was underage.

The day came for me to go for my physical. I lived in Levelland, but I had orders to go to Brownfield, Texas, about thirty miles away and from there, we would be taken by bus to Amarillo for the physical. I was physically strong and had played sports in school and so we all felt that I would pass my physical and be taken away. At that time, the Viet Nam war was going on. I just knew that I would be sent to Viet Nam.

My Father drove me to Brownfield to the bus station and dropped me off. I do not remember if anyone else went with us. I got on the bus that was waiting to take us to Amarillo.

We got to Amarillo to the place where I was to have the physical and were all herded into a big class room. We were given forms to fill out that would provide Uncle Sam with lots of information. After that was completed we were all taken into another big room and given all kinds of instructions. We were assigned lockers and ordered to remove our clothes down to our underwear.

After we had stripped down to our underwear we were instructed to form a single line and were taken through a series of tests. We were weighed and our height was measured. The next room was for vision and hearing.

As I was tested for hearing, I was told to place the earphones over my ears and instructed to press the button when I stopped hearing the sound. I followed instructions.

When we were through testing for hearing, then I was checked for vision. I had worn glasses since I was in the fifth grade. I knew my vision was bad because I could not see much in distance without my glasses. Then I had to try to read some numbers that I could not make out. The man who was testing my eyes asked me if I knew how long I had been color blind. I told him that I was not color blind. He repeated the test. He then said that the test results showed that I was color blind. He asked me to wait there.

He returned with another man dressed in Army uniform. The man dressed in Army uniform told me to read out some numbers that again, I could not see. The man then told me to take care of my eyes because I might go blind by the age of forty. He also asked about my trouble hearing. I told him I did not have any trouble hearing. He told me I had problems with my hearing. He did not seem to be a nice man.

The first man who had first checked my eyes told me to follow him. They took me into a room where there were a few others that had come on the same bus. I was told to get dressed and to wait there. I got dressed and sat there waiting. Finally a man came and took us to a waiting room. I was told I had not passed my physical exam. We were told to wait for the rest of the other young men that had come with us on the bus. Then we were all told to get on the bus and we would be going back to Brownfield.

They fed us at noon, but now it was about five in the afternoon. When we got to Brownfield I had nowhere to go and no phone number to call. I did not know the town and it was thirty miles to Levelland.

There happened to be two young men on the bus who had also failed their physicals and I had over heard them mention Levelland several times. I asked them if they were from Levelland and they said yes. I asked them if I could ride back with them and the driver said yes. They were nice, about my age and by the way they talked, they liked having a good time. Drinking was one of the things they enjoyed.

The three of us got into a 1959 Ford. The two young men were in the front and I was in the back seat by myself. The driver and the other young man were laughing at what they had done the night before at a going away party held for them. Apparently their family and friends thought they would be getting into the Army. The two kept talking about the surprise they had for their friends since they had failed their physical.

Once we were out of the Brownfield city limits, the driver pressed on the gas paddle. The radio was playing a little too loud and they kept talking about the fun they had had at the party. We kept going faster and faster. I started to pray. The car speedometer kept going higher and higher. Then it was up to ninety miles per hour. I continued to pray.

The two young men were laughing and having so much fun at ninety miles an hour. I was petrified with fear. It did not matter now whether I had passed or failed my Army physical. I was going to die. I did not know whether the car had good tires or not. I prayed that a highway patrol would see us and stop us. I had never been in a car that had gone past fifty five miles an hour, much less ninety miles an hour.

My Lord in heaven takes good care of all of us who are crazy, who are idiots, stupid and in-between. I don't know which one I was, but the guardian angels stayed busy protecting us, even if they, themselves, were at risk. All those years and times I had prayed had been helpful because I knew how to pray, and I prayed. I'm sure my whole life passed right before my eyes but we were going so fast, I did not get to see it.

Finally, from a distance, we saw the lights from the town of Levelland. The driver slowed down because, as he said, he did not want to get a speeding ticket. He did not think about that at ninety miles an hour. Go figure. They dropped me off and drove off. I am not sure they heard my thank you. Or maybe I did not say thank you. I was alive. I was at home. I stopped praying.

My wife, parents, and all other friends and relatives were very happily surprised that I had not passed the physical exam. My Mother cried. Me, I was just damned happy to be alive. I have never told anyone about the ride that night, until now, because I was just happy to be alive.

At the beginning of the school year, it felt odd that I no longer had to go to school. I went to work different places. I did not try working at the bank because I had found out after completing my business school that I did not like working with numbers.

Margie and I went back to Melvin. I did not have a job in Melvin and did not know what to do as far as work. We moved to Brownwood.

In Brownwood, I worked washing dishes while I looked for a job. A short time later I got a job working at a meat packing company. It was even harder work than working in the fields. But I had to work. I was married now.

After working there a while, I was offered a job working the night shift at the meat packing company cleaning the equipment used by the people working the day shift. It was not the best job, but pay was good and it was much easier than the day job.

I had really liked Abilene, Texas, when I lived there while going to business school. So we moved to Abilene. I was able to get a job working in the cafeteria at the hospital. I did not know what profession I wanted to pursue, which seemed dumb being that I was married. Frankly, I am not too sure I knew how to work. I was a very good worker at whatever work I did. But I did not know what I wanted to do as far as work. I also went to work at a nursing home as an orderly, as they called male nurse aides. We did all the dirty work. I found myself coasting along with jobs I did not really like and that did not pay well.

CHAPTER 16

MY DAUGHTER IS BORN

Margie became pregnant and I had to pay for the doctor and hospital bills. I did not have any insurance so I paid for the cost of the hospital and doctor prior to delivery. It was very hard for us, but we were both used to being poor. Boy we struggled. I was the only one working and I had a car that would take me to work if it felt like it.

Margie went into labor and we went to the hospital. She was placed in the labor room and I was allowed to be there with her. I would not be allowed to be in the delivery room. Back then, husbands could not be in the delivery rooms. But having husbands present in the labor room was enough trouble for the nurses. If other husbands acted like I did in the labor room, anyone could understand that rule.

A nurse came into the waiting room and told me I could go into the labor room and be with my wife. I was happy to be there at Margie's bedside, at least through the labor part. We did not know yet what gender the baby would be. Back then, we learned the gender at the time of the birth. Older women I knew used to say that if the pregnant mother's stomach was pointed (not as round, I guess) the baby would be a boy. If the mother's stomach was round the baby would be a girl. Old wives tales.

The nurse came into the room with a bell. The nurse asked me if I could ring the bell when my wife started a contraction. I said yes, I would ring the bell. The nurse stated that she wanted to time the frequency of the contractions. Of course, anybody can do that. She told me she would be right down the hall and would be right over if I rang the bell. She thanked me and left the door ajar behind her. As soon as she left, I walked over to the side of the bed.

As I neared the bedside Margie made a moaning sound. I rang the bell. The nurse was there right away. She asked Margie if she was having contractions and if they were very strong. Margie said she was not having a contraction. The nurse then turned to me and instructed me to ring the bell only if it was a contraction. Never having known anything about birthing babies, I nodded my head as in understanding the instructions.

The nurse walked out, again leaving the door ajar as she had done before. I walked to the bedside and called out to Margie. She moaned and I rang the bell. The nurse was there almost instantly. After the nurse assessed my wife and established there had been no contraction, the nurse grabbed the bell and stated, looking at me, not smiling, "You don't need this." She walked out leaving the door ajar, but taking the bell with her.

Finally it was time for Margie to go into the delivery room. My mother-in-law and I waited in the waiting room until a nurse came and told me I had a daughter. On June 25, 1966, my daughter was born. The nurse then walked us to a window where I could see my baby daughter. The nurse that brought my daughter to the window for me to see smiled as she showed me my daughter. My daughter was wiggling, making faces, ugly little faces.

I was taken to the room where Margie was and I was told I could only be there for a few minutes. And a few minutes it was. My mother-in-law and I went home. I went to the hospital next day and was able to hold my little daughter. Margie and I were both happy to have our little girl. We named our baby daughter Nelda Ann. My oldest sister had suggested the name and we both agreed.

As we talked about taking the baby home, we both realized that we had not bought baby clothes. We had nothing for the baby. You see, we had been told by both my mother and my mother-in-law that it was not good to buy clothes for the baby before the baby is born because the baby may not live. I have no idea where our mothers came up with that but the worst part was that we believed it. I prefer to say that I was naïve rather than stupid. I know what everyone else thinks. That's okay. The Lord loves us all, naïve or stupid. But we did enjoy buying clothes for the baby when we could.

Having Nelda was fun. I had someone to love and take care of, to protect and make sure that all went well with her. Margie was a wonderful, loving and caring mother to our daughter.

Nelda was a fun baby. She learned fast and it was fun teaching her to walk. Margie and I would sit on the floor a few feet apart and have Nelda walk back and forth to each other. We encouraged her each time she would fall on her behind or if she just sat down afraid to continue.

Nelda also spent a lot of time with my parents. My Father spoiled her. As time went on, I saw that Nelda was one of his favorite grandchildren. My Father had favorite grandchildren. My Mother loved all her grandchildren equally.

Margie and I, with our daughter, had our good times. Margie and I did not argue. Margie never asked for anything more than what I could provide. But I had my bad times. I had times when I felt lonely, times when I felt that I was still bad and that I did not deserve to be loved. I thought that I could forget the past once I got away from all the reminders of Old Grandfather. I felt that I was worthless and no good. I had not seen Old Grandfather for several years now, but funny how the mind works. The things that happened with Old Grandfather never went away. The feelings of being worthless, of always feeling that others were better than I was kept coming back.

My life was strange. Strange in that I felt I was three different persons. One person was a husband, father and sometimes happy. Another person was one who felt worthless, no good, dirty, and still another one that felt alone and lonely.

CHAPTER 17

THE BEGINNING OF MY CAREER

In April of 1967, my Mother was admitted to the Brady hospital for surgery. I took my vacation time to help out while my Mother was in the hospital. My Mother would have to stay at least two weeks in the hospital after her surgery. I stayed with my Mother at night to help her if she needed anything. My sisters stayed during the day. Margie and I were staying at my parent's house.

One morning while I was in the hospital room with my Mother a nurse came by and asked me if I ever thought about going to nursing school. The nurse told me that I did a very good job of taking care of my sick mother. I said no. I had always hated hospitals, could not stand the sight of blood, and feared needles. She told me that the nursing school there at the hospital was having an entrance exam that morning and suggested that I take the exam. She told me I did not have to go to nursing school, but that if I decided to, I would have already taken the exam. So I took the exam. I did well on my exam and I was in. That fast.

I told my parents that I wanted to go to nursing school. My Mother told me to go to nursing school and that Margie, Nelda and I could live with them while I went to school. Brady was only 16 miles from Melvin. And that is what I did.

I started the Licensed Vocational Nursing School in Brady in August of 1968. I was one of two male students starting the nursing class. I do not remember how many of us started the nursing program that year, but there were only six of us students in the class that graduated from the nursing program.

At that time I did not have a car. My old 1954 Ford had broken down for good. My Father let me use his car three weeks a month because he car-pooled with three men that he worked with. On the week that my father used his car for car-pool, I would stay at the hospital. Margie would bring me work clothes in the middle of the week. It was extremely hard for me to go to school, to work and not have a car. But I kept on going to school.

I received help from several people. The director of the nursing school program, who was also the director of nurses at the hospital, helped me have a place to sleep when I could not go home from school. I would sleep in a vacant room at the hospital or in a room in the old building that was used as the class room. The school building was actually an old house behind the hospital building. Nursing students would walk across the parking lot to and from the school building to the hospital when attending classes or completing the hands-on patient care training.

The nursing program paid the students a monthly stipend which was not much but helped greatly. If I remember correctly, the stipend was ninety dollars a month. I also know that it was a great help to some of the other students. I also worked on weekends at the hospital so that I could make extra money. The director of nurses knew that I needed to work as much as I could so she would assign me to work when she needed someone to fill in at the hospital.

During this year on July 20, 1969, the United States landed on the moon. I remember looking at the television showing the landing and listening to what the astronauts were saying. This was all interesting to me and to millions of others that got to watch the event take place.

Not having to pay rent was a great help. My parents were really nice to allow me with my family to live with them. I had hoped that living with my parents would be only temporary and I told myself that it would be. Temporary turned out to be a full year.

As hard as it was for me to go to nursing school, the one year of nursing school went by fast. I was finally finished with the nursing program. I graduated from the nursing program in August, 1969. After graduation, I went to Austin, Texas, to take the state board exam for licensure. I passed the exam and I became a Licensed Vocational Nurse (LVN). At last, I could finally work and make some money to rent a house, pay the bills and buy a car.

I continued working at the Brady hospital after I acquired my license. We rented a house in Brady that belonged to a husband and wife that had lived in town but were now living at their ranch. The husband had been a patient at the hospital where I worked and I had told him I was looking for a house to rent in Brady. He then told me about the house they owned in Brady and that they would rent it to us. He told me he would rent the house to us for thirty five dollars a month on the condition that he and his wife could come over on Sundays and use the house. They had to come into town to buy groceries and do other errands and they would use the house to rest while they were in town. Margie and I felt that it was a great deal and so we moved to Brady.

The house was huge, as it seemed to us. It had a large front porch, large parking space in front of the house, pecan trees around the house. Nelda could play on the porch. The landlord had left the washer and dryer. His wife would do laundry sometimes on the Sundays when they came to town. We were told to use the washer and dryer.

A cousin of mine lived behind the house we had moved into. My cousin and her husband were friends of the landlord and his wife. My cousin was happy to have us move into the house. She said that now she could have someone to visit. She also had a grandson that she would baby sit during the day. He was the same age as my daughter, so they learned to play together. And the house was close to the hospital. It would make it easy for me to go to work.

So it was great for us. Margie stayed at home and took care of Nelda. My parents would come in from Melvin and visit and at times, would take Nelda back to Melvin with them. Nelda seemed to enjoy being with them and, of course, they enjoyed having Nelda with them.

There were windows in the bedroom that we could leave open at night. Because the days were still hot, a beautiful breeze would blow in through the windows at night.

We could sleep very comfortable without having to use the air conditioner.

This particular night, we got ready to go to bed as usual. We had the windows open and I turned off the light as I got into bed. I lay my head on the pillow when suddenly we heard the most awful sound just outside the bedroom window behind the head of our bed. There is no way anyone can ever mistake that sound. Even if you have never heard it before, you would know what that sound was. A dog kept barking just outside the window where the sound came from. The sound kept getting louder and then suddenly we hear the dog yelp.

The dog ran off yelping and then the sound stopped. There was no mistaking it. That was a rattlesnake and it had to be a large snake. The sound had come from right outside the bedroom window. The next day we told my cousin that lived behind our house. She and her husband told us to call the landlord and let him know. The landlord used to attend rattlesnake roundups and used to have a large round aluminum water trough in the garage. He would capture live rattlesnakes and put them in the aluminum water trough and then take the rattlesnakes to the roundup.

When I told the landlord what we heard, he instructed us to stay inside the house, not to let Nelda play in the yard and if we walked from the driveway to the house in the dark, to walk in the middle of the sidewalk. He also told me that he would come in on Sunday and remove the rattlesnake.

On Sunday morning the landlord and his wife came to our house as usual. The owner put a head light on and took a long pole with a cord tied to one end of the pole.

At the end of the pole was a clamp that could be opened by pulling on the cord. He then went under the house and instructed us to move back away from the opening when we saw him coming out. We did as he instructed.

After what seemed about thirty minutes, we saw his feet coming out through the opening leading under the house. We all moved back. We could hear the sound of the rattlesnake as he came out and dragged the pole out from under the house. At the end of the pole, which had the clamp attached to it, was a large rattlesnake.

The owner then went on to show us how strong the snake was. He grabbed a yardstick and moved it towards the head of the snake. With lightning speed the snake struck at the yardstick. The owner then showed us where the snake had struck the yard stick. The snake continued to strike but the clamp held it back. The owner then killed the snake. He then told us that we could feel safe now. He said he had checked under the house and did not find any other snakes.

From then on we did not let Nelda walk on the grass or play outside by herself. We made it a point to not have to walk outside unless absolutely necessary. We were afraid. We thought of all the times that we let Nelda and my cousin's grandson play outside. We thought of what could have happened to the two, three-year-olds. I thanked God for keeping our two young children safe.

My mother-in-law and her two young sons lived in Abilene. We would visit them when we could. One of the times that we visited in Abilene, I went and inquired about the pay scale at a hospital in Abilene. The hospital was new and when I talked to the Human Resource person in charge, she told me they were hiring and in need of nurses.

The amount of pay that was quoted was almost twice as much as I was earning in Brady.

Margie and I decided that we would move to Abilene where I could get work at the hospital and get better pay. I went back to the new hospital in Abilene and completed my application. I was hired immediately and was given the time I needed to give my two weeks' notice in Brady and move to Abilene. So I gave my notice and we moved to Abilene.

In Abilene we lived with my mother-in-law until we could find a place to live. We drove around looking for a place to rent when we saw a house that was for sale. We had never talked about buying a house but we stopped and looked at the house. We immediately fell in love with the house. It was nothing fancy, just a simple wooden house in what appeared to be a nice neighborhood and an elementary school at the end of the street. We felt it was perfect for us. We bought the house.

The house turned out to be just perfect for us. It was convenient for us in every respect. We started to buy furniture, a little at a time. I was the only one working at this time so we could only afford one cheap piece of furniture at a time. But we liked our house and everything seemed to be going good for us. I was working at the hospital on the night shift.

I hated working the night shift. I could not sleep during the day, or if I slept, I would sleep from the time I got home until it was time for me to go back to work. When I went to request for a position on the day shift, I was told that they did not have any openings. So I kept on working the night shift.

After working at that hospital for about a year, I started hearing rumors of possibly the hospital having financial problems. I decided to apply for work at Hendricks hospital, the largest hospital in Abilene. I was hired for the day shift. I gave my notice at my current place of employment and made my second job change in two years.

Working at Hendricks hospital was good for me. Work was hard, but I learned a lot about new procedures, diagnosis, treatments, and new nursing procedures. I enjoyed the people I worked with except for two nurses that worked on the same unit I worked.

One of the nurses was grouchy. The other nurses always seemed to give excuses on her behalf as to why she was like that and, I guess, why it was acceptable. I finally got tired of her being ugly to me and I asked her what her problem was. I told her that I had a right to come to work and not have to be treated in the manner she was treating me. Her grouchiness stopped and it became comfortable working with her.

The other nurse was different. She had a higher position, which was being in charge when the head nurse was off. She reported me to the supervisor so often that it eventually became sort of a joke with the other nurses. The director of nurses once told us that we, the charge nurse and I, spent more time in her office than on the floor working. Never the less, it never really got good between us, even though we did continue working together.

There was a change of head nurse on our unit and our unit was moved to the top floor of a new wing that had been added to the hospital. Both head nurses, the one that left and the new one that was brought to our unit were very nice. They were both very good nurses and very good at management.

CHAPTER **18**

MY SON IS BORN

By now Margie and I had decided to have another baby. I was the only one working and maybe not financially ready to have another baby, but as it turned out, no regrets. This would have been our third child. Margie had a miscarriage during the first few months of her second pregnancy. I will never forget that we would have had another little girl. But it was not meant to be. God knows why things happen.

This time we had a boy. I wanted to, and did name our son David Raymond. All of the closest friends I ever had were named David, so we named our son David. David had a full head of black hair when he was born. By the age of three months, he received his first haircut. I was very proud of him. I am sure that Margie was very proud of him also, but I will only speak for myself.

We were prepared for our son's birth financially and as far as having baby clothes and diapers. We had gone through one bad experience with Nelda and we decided that we would not make the same mistake twice. We tried to have plenty of baby clothes and even had a special outfit we used to bring him home from the hospital.

We had the baby crib that Nelda had used, except with a new mattress, ready for him. The baby crib had been given to us by some family friends of ours that lived in Abilene. They were very nice to give us the baby crib. They saw how badly we needed the crib and how we could not afford to buy one. Nelda outgrew the baby crib and we had saved it for future use.

After David was born, we became a normal family living a normal family life, doing what families are supposed to do. There again, what is a normal family life? We had a house, a car, friends, went to church, and visited our families. I guess that is what normal is and what normal people do. Margie did not know how to drive so I had to drive her to the grocery store, sometimes to work, and any other place she needed to go. I kept encouraging her to drive, but she was not ready to learn.

Margie got a job at the Timex factory which was located close to downtown Abilene. Working at the Timex factory, Margie was off every weekend and on holidays. I on the other hand, worked nearly every weekend and holidays. I was working at the hospital and my work schedule was to work six days and off two days. With this schedule, most of my days off were during the week. We did not get to do very much as a family on weekends. And because money was tight, I very frequently volunteered to work extra. We needed the money.

Nelda was now old enough to go to head start. I worked the evening shift for a while, so I would walk her to the elementary school that was located at the end of the block where we lived. The school bus would pick up the children and bus them to another part of town where they attended head start.

As soon as Nelda got on the bus, I would drive to the school where she would attend head start. I would park my car across the street and wait for the bus to come by and drop off the children. I would watch Nelda get off the bus along with the other children and go into her class room. I was satisfied then that she was okay. Then I would drive home and wait for time for me to go to work. I don't remember how long I kept that up but eventually I stopped following the school bus to the other side of town to make sure Nelda got there safely. Actually, I got tired of doing that. I also realized how dumb that was. So I only walked her to the school down the street and once she got on the school bus, I would go home.

The time went by and so did the years. The children grew up really fast. I watched my children grow up through the elementary school years and then through junior high or what we now refer to as middle school.

I remember that the children growing up were very good years for me. I got to do fun things with them. They learned to skate and the whole family would go skating. Nelda was a very good skater. I later got to the point where I would not skate with them but would bring Nelda's little friends along to skate with her. I would sit and watch them skate, very proud to see my children enjoy themselves.

Even though I was a licensed nurse, I always thought I might want to do something else. Like the time I thought

I wanted to be a barber. I think my son was about six years old when I decided to learn to cut hair. I had cut my sister's hair and it had turned out pretty good. David had straight hair and wore it somewhat longish with bangs like the Beatles' hair style. I came up with the brilliant idea to give him a haircut.

I placed a chair in the middle of the room and a pillow on the chair and told my son to kneel on the pillow facing the back rest of the chair. I placed a towel around his neck and shoulders and started cutting. After several minutes David became restless and started fidgeting. I got upset with him for moving and told him to stay still. When he would get tired we would take a break and then continue the haircut.

After about an hour or so, my son started to complain about not feeling well. I kept cutting his hair. Suddenly he started shaking and sliding to one side. He was passing out. I am a licensed nurse, but I froze. I could not move to help my son. Nelda was lying on the sofa this whole time talking and watching me cut hair. She got up, got a hold of David and helped him to the sofa and laid him down. I stood there and watched but did not move. After a few minutes, David started talking and seemed to be alright. He said he just could not breathe from being in that position for so long. I gave up the idea of becoming a barber.

Margie and the children were happy. We had fun times as a family and Nelda and David enjoyed their friends. But all was not well with me. I had everything any man would long to have. But there was that part inside of me that I hated and wished I could forget.

Old Grandfather was already gone. My Mother called us one day to let me know that Old Grandfather had died. Since my Mother did not know about Old Grandfather and me, I guess she probably felt I might be sad. Hearing the news was a great relief to me and I was actually happy. I did believe my Mother that the old man was dead, but I had to see it for myself. I wanted to be sure he had died. So I went to Melvin to see with my own eyes.

At last I could close that part of my life and never think about it again. I had never told anyone and now I could just forget everything and never deal with it again.

But it just does not work out that way. Some memories cannot be erased or forgotten. I still felt that I was a bad person and that I did not deserve to be loved. I felt that it had been my fault for allowing those bad things to happen to me. After all this years, everything that had happened with Old Grandfather still would go through my mind. I kept feeling that I was worthless.

All this time, instead of forgetting, it kept creeping into my mind with frequency. Why had I allowed him to do that to me? I would tell myself that I deserved feeling bad for not fighting him, for not running away from him, for not doing something. I wish I knew why. Why me? How had I encouraged Old Grandfather to do that to me? I kept trying to figure out why it was my fault. And so I kept everything to myself.

The other part of me also kept resurfacing. I thought about men. Whenever I saw a nice looking man, I felt good about him. I wanted to stare. Not every man made me feel that way so I told myself that there was nothing to it. Besides, I was a married man with a beautiful wife and two wonderful children. I was not supposed to experience those feelings. That stirred up more bad feelings towards me. I was an awful person. I could not shake that feeling out of my mind.

I continued working at the hospital and worked as much extra time at the hospital as I could. I also worked part time at a nursing home, usually the night shift. Working as many hours as I did was not that bad. I was young and I could do it. The only bad thing was that it took me away from my family. But we needed the money.

My children were growing and I wanted them to have everything I did not have when growing up. I wanted to be a better provider than my Father had been. I wanted my children to experience so much more than I had. All I had done while growing up was work hard. But there again, I felt that the hard work had taught me to be responsible and a good provider. And I was those things.

But my past would always come to haunt me. The past was always there. Old Grandfather had died and he was in the past. Or was he? At times I felt very alone, very lonely. Those are two different things, and I was experiencing both and with more frequency.

I always kept my feelings so well hidden that people that knew me did not know how I felt and what I was going through. Work was my good friend. I did not have time to think when working.

CHAPTER 19

WORKING AT THE HOSPITAL

I enjoyed working at the hospital and I was a very good nurse. I cared about my patients and would try to help the families as much as I could. There were so many good things for me to be happy about in working at the hospital. Patients appreciated what I did for them and the families also seemed to appreciate me.

I am sure that if you ask any nurse that has worked in a hospital, that nurse will have a lot of stories to tell about the good, and the not so good experiences. And I also have a lot of stories I could tell from working in the hospital. A story I will tell is the one that inspired me to write a poem.

The unit or floor, as we used to refer to it, was on the seventh floor of the hospital. The registered nurse in charge of the unit and all the nurses that worked on that unit were some of the greatest nurses I have ever had the privilege to work with.

The head nurse was very intelligent, caring, and a great leader. She was the calmest person during emergencies. Nothing seemed to rattle her. Whatever emergency we had on our unit, she would stay calm and would smile and be nice to you, and teach. And she did all this while she took care of the emergency.

She would come to work in the mornings in her white nurse's uniform, spotless white shoes, and every hair in place. When she went home late afternoon, her uniform would be just as spotless as when she had come to work in the morning, her shoes as spotless and every hair still in place. When she was in charge, everything would run smoothly. We all felt calm, sure of ourselves, enjoyed work, and we laughed a lot during the day. When she had the day off, our day at work was not so smooth.

Going back to my nurse story, every morning after we got the report from the nurse finishing the night shift, our charge nurse would make the assignments for those of us working the day shift. We would then go out on the floor, make rounds, take the patient's vital signs (temperature, pulse, respirations, and blood pressure), pass out the breakfast trays, pass out the morning medications and pass out the linen packs that contained the linens that would be used to change the patients' beds. During this time of day, there would be a lot of traffic going on in the unit. There would be patients on stretchers going to surgery or wheelchairs going to x-ray. Some doctors would also be on the unit making their rounds. So the mornings were usually very chaotic.

This particular morning I had been assigned to a middle age, male patient who had come in to the hospital for tests.

The patient's doctor had made his visit early this morning and had given the patient the results of the tests.

The door was ajar so I knocked lightly and walked in. I said good morning as I walked to his bedside. He did not respond or turn his head to look at me. I noticed the head of his bed was raised in a half-way sitting position, his bedside table was pushed aside near the bed, and the bright morning sun light was shining through the window onto his face. He was looking out the window with his hands clasped together in front of him on his lap. As the sun shined on his face I could see the reflection of the sparkling of the tears.

The doctor had informed him that the results of the tests indicated he had terminal cancer. What do you say to someone at a time like that? I stood at his bedside and held his hand. I stood there for what seemed to be a long time but it was actually maybe a minute or two. When he could speak, he turned his head and looked at me and said, "Thank you." and squeezed my hand.

And so I wrote the following poem.

Warm sunlight thru the window
Awakens him to another day.
The hustle and bustle of all different people,
All different moods.
Some understanding, some indifferent.
Doing their duties, rushing the day.
But, for him—
Do we prolong the day:
What is he feeling?
What is his care?
A friendly "good morning"---

Yet, For him, it is an ending,
Ever so near.
On his face, I see a sparkle,
A sparkle---
That of a tear.

Another nurse story: There was the time when, because we were on the highest floor of the hospital wing, someone decided that the portable defibrillator should be kept on our floor. If there was a "code blue" (cardiac arrest) on any of the floors below our floor, a nurse from our unit was to grab the portable defibrillator and run down the stairs to the floor and to the room where the emergency was located. The portable defibrillator was too heavy for one person, so we were instructed that two nurses would carry the defibrillator to the emergency location.

On the first code blue that was called through the intercom system when I was on duty, a young nurse and I grabbed the defibrillator and started running down the stairs. We were both running as fast as we could, one of us on each side holding on to the defibrillator. We ran down about two flights of stairs when the nurse tells me to stop. I said no, we needed to hurry. She then informed me that her panty hose were rolling down to her thighs. She told me to wait just a second. She then pulled her panty hose up and we continued running down the stairs. We had to stop three times for her to pull her panty hose up.

We got the defibrillator to the room, but we were laughing so hard, we almost did not make it to the floor where the defibrillator was needed. Eventually, the hospital changed their rules and we no longer had to run with the defibrillator to other units below us.

The hospital also had Diploma Registered Nurses (RN) and License Vocational Nurses (LVN) nursing schools. Many of the nursing students stayed and worked at Hendricks Hospital after graduation. The men and women that graduated from either of the nursing programs made great nurses. The charge nurse of the unit I worked on had graduated from the RN school. And she was fantastic. Very few graduates, and I mean very few, did not make good nurses. We had one of the very few on our unit, but I won't go there.

We always enjoyed having the nursing students come to our unit and help take care of the patients, which was part of their training. It would be a great help to us on the floor and it was great experience for the students. Students going through the training were so naïve. And we would laugh at some of the things they said and did, but at the same time we tried to help them.

One day one of the students came to the nurse's station where I was doing documentation on a patient's clinical record. The student's patient had been discharged and had gone home. The student had a pair of house shoes that the patient had forgotten. She asked me what she should do with the house shoes. I told her to put them in one of the shelves behind the nurses' station and when we had enough items collected, we would have a garage sale. So she placed them on the shelf as instructed and I forgot about the whole thing. I had only been joking.

Several weeks later, the head nurse was looking for some type of medical equipment and she opened the door to the shelves behind the nurses' station. She asked loudly and in surprise, "What on earth is this?" We all quickly went to see what she was talking about. All the shelves were packed full of items, like house shoes, clothing, toiletries, etc. We had no idea what was going on, why all that stuff was there.

Strangely enough, that same afternoon, a few hours after the discovery of the stuffed shelves, about four nursing students walked up to the nurses' station with arms loaded with paper bags full of stuff. The charge nurse smiled and said hi and asked them what they had in their paper bags. One student announced so proudly that they had gone around gathering unwanted items and would like to donate to the garage sale we were having. The student went on, "We have being gathering stuff and storing them on the shelves, but I don't think there is room for all these other bags. Joe told us that you had garage sales and we wanted to help."

All eyes turned to look at me. There was complete silence. The charge nurse smiled and told the students that was very nice of them, told them to set the bags on the floor in the conference room, and told them that we did not need any more things. We had enough. They sat the bags on the floor and happy with their contribution, they walked away. I do not remember what happened to the items that were brought by the students for the garage sale, but I know they were not thrown away. We all laughed about the incident, but I really felt bad about it.

My other nurse story: When I worked at the hospital, I always wanted to learn new procedures, or anything new pertaining to nursing. So I was very excited when the charge nurse instructed me to go to central supply and bring a tray for a procedure that the doctor was going to perform on a patient in the patient's room. The doctor was going to perform a chest puncture on a patient and remove fluid from the chest cavity. I had never seen this procedure done and I was very interested in learning about the procedure and to get to

146

see the procedure being done. I had informed the head nurse that I had never seen this procedure being done and she said she would be there to assist the doctor and I could observe.

The procedure had been explained to the patient and the doctor, the head nurse and I were ready to proceed with the procedure. My responsibility was to place the drainage tube in the container sitting on the floor into which the fluid would be draining. The doctor explained some of the procedure to me and made sure I could see how the procedure was being done. I was so intent on watching what the doctor was doing that I forgot about the drainage tube. When I looked down to check on the drainage tube, I saw that the drainage tube was stuck inside the cuff of the doctor's pants. I quickly place the drainage tube in the drainage bottle and continued to observe the procedure. I found the whole procedure very fascinating and I did not want to miss any part of the procedure.

When the doctor was finished with the procedure, I was instructed to carry the bottle of fluid to the lab. While I was labeling the bottle, I heard the doctor and the head nursing talking about the patient. Then I heard the doctor tell the head nurse that he did not know why his shoe was wet. He stated that his sock was also wet. Then he said, "Oh well, I need to be in O.R. I will take my shoes off then." And he left. I carried the bottle with the fluid to the lab and got back to the unit.

I worried the whole time about having to tell the head nurse what had happened but when I got to the floor, I told the head nurse. She knew how badly I felt and she tried to keep a straight face, but not for long. She told me that we had gotten enough fluid for the analysis and the doctor's shoe and sock were not that wet.

Eventually I was transferred to the fifth floor which was a cardiac floor. I did not have as much fun working there as I had on the seventh floor, but the nurses were nice. I missed working with the nurses on the seventh floor. I did get to tell the charge nurse that I thought she was the best nurse there was and that if some day I became a registered nurse, if I was at least half as good as she was, I would be a great nurse.

I worked every day I was scheduled to work, missing work only when I was sick. I was getting paid about four dollars and seventy-five cents an hour. That required me to work on my days off as often as they could use me, which they always did. I was young and enjoyed my work so I did not mind the work. I just wished I could have been getting paid more.

In 1974, I decided I wanted to become a registered nurse. I started taking classes at a community college that was about fifty miles from Abilene. There were three of us taking the classes so that we could enroll in the registered nurse program at the hospital where I worked. The three of us going to the classes would take turns driving to the college. I was able to attend college for one semester.

Towards the end of the first semester, my car broke. It was the transmission. The mechanic estimated it would cost about four to five hundred dollars to repair. I completed the semester but could not continue going to school. I got a second job at a nursing home working the evening shift and sometimes the night shift. I worked from seven a.m. to three thirty p.m. at the hospital then rushed to the nursing home and worked until eleven p.m. It was rough working both jobs but I got my car repaired. After I repaired my car, I went back to working only at the hospital, but working as much overtime as I could.

CHAPTER 20

MY CHILDREN

My daughter was in middle school now and had become a beautiful young lady. I remember her first report card after she had started middle school. They were low, bad, pitiful grades. Her two little Hispanic girl friends that were sisters and lived across the street had also brought home bad grades. Nelda also had another two little white girl friends, not related to each other, which lived down the street and both had the same name. Those two white little girls brought home straight A's.

I remember I sat my daughter down and asked her if she felt that both those little white girls were better than her. She said no. I then asked her why the little white girls had straight A's and she and the two sisters across the street had low grades. All five girls were nearly always together. Why was there so much difference? I told her that if she was doing the best she could, I could understand, but if she was not, she needed to make sure that she was trying her best. I knew my daughter was a leader, as I paid attention and noticed that her friends would follow her. I knew she could do a lot better. I was hoping that talking to her would make her try to do better at school.

Well, it worked. Her next report card had improved tremendously. She had even made some A's. I told her I was very proud of her and told her I knew she could do it. From then on her grades were great. She made the National Junior Honor Society in her ninth grade year. She also played sports and I felt she was good at it. I was extremely proud of her.

On August 9, 1974, President Richard Nixon resigned as President of the United States. He was the first President to resign from the presidency. Again I sat in front of the television listening to President Nixon as he gave his resignation speech.

I worked hard to provide for my children. As I may have mentioned before, I wanted my children to have things that I never had while growing up. I did not want them to miss out on experiencing things I never got to experience because we were always so poor. I wanted them to have the money to be able to go to a football game or basketball game and not have to "sneak in over the fence". I wanted my children to have nice clothes, have their own bedrooms, plenty of food, and have shoes without holes in the soles. I guess most fathers want the same things for their children.

Nelda was a very private person, and still is. She never complained about things. She did not ask for much. When she was sick, she never let us know she was not feeling well. She would stay in her room and that would be how we knew something was wrong. Nelda was a worker and still is. As soon as she was able, age wise, she got a job at a clothing store. She worked the summers and sometimes during Christmas breaks from school.

Nelda was also popular. She always had friends with her. The two sisters that lived across the street were always coming over to the house or Nelda going over to their house. But they were very good kids. There were also many other friends that Nelda had. I took notice of her friends. They were all nice kids and I was very proud of Nelda for choosing her friends well.

My son, David, was a very good boy growing up. I did not have many problems from him. He also had some little neighbor friends who went to school with him. David seemed to enjoy playing with his little friends that lived two houses down from us. We felt comfortable allowing David to go play at their house and we allowed the little boys to come and play with David at our house.

One day David brought home a note from his first or second grade teacher. She wanted to talk to us. I had to work so Margie went to talk to the teacher. The teacher had given Margie a tablet with a word that my son had printed in big letters on the front of the tablet. The four letter word started with "f" and ended with "k". I asked him if he knew what the word meant and he said no, but his little friend had written that word in the front of his writing tablet so he felt he wanted to write that word also.

Oh, oh, my son is a follower. I had to talk to him also otherwise, he would be getting in trouble doing things just because others did. I talked to him then, but I was not too sure if he understood. I had to wait and see.

For some reason, David did not seem to want to go to school. He would hide and the teachers would have to look for him. It scared the teachers and it scared me. We tried to find out why he was doing that, but did not seem to get any direct straight answer. Eventually he quit hiding and went to school without us worrying.

I remember feeling that I wanted to protect David and I did not know how or why I should protect him. Often I would think of him when I was alone and I would cry. I do not know why I would cry. I just saw him so innocent, such a handsome little boy.

As a family we attended the St. Vincent Palloti Catholic Church. The nun would use our house one day a week after school to teach the young children that attended the elementary school at the end of our street. The nun would stay and eat with us and then she would leave.

Finally, it was time for David to receive his First Communion sacrament. Normally for First Communion, the parents of the child would ask a close friend or family member to be their child's sponsor. In the old days when I was growing up, that was a big event to receive the First Communion sacrament. The sponsor would be someone dear to the parents and afterwards, the parents of the child and the sponsor would be "compadres". Margie and I decided that I would be David's sponsor. And I was. My son received his sacrament and I was right there with him. We dressed almost alike. We wore khaki pants and yellow shirts. And I had an afro. I will always remember that.

My children and I would do things together and I enjoyed that. We laughed a lot. They were always doing funny things. Like the time Nelda was babysitting for the neighbor's one-year-old baby boy. The day was hot and the little boy was asleep on the couch wearing only a diaper. Nelda was in the kitchen doing something. I heard David call Nelda to check on the baby. I also went to check and see what was going on with the baby. David was standing near the door and I understood why. He had covered the baby with lotion and baby powder all over his body. Nelda was angry but couldn't keep from laughing. Nelda chased David out of the house but did not seem to be trying to catch him. Nelda and I were both laughing. The baby woke up later after Nelda had gotten through cleaning him up.

Nelda and David were close. Margie and I never had problems with them fighting with each other. Nelda sometimes seemed protective of David. And when growing up, if David got hurt and cried, he would go to Nelda for consoling instead of going to Margie or coming to me.

One time I told them they should mow yards to make money. They found a yard to mow and I took them in my car and dropped them off with the lawn mower. It was a small yard and I felt they would be okay. When I drove by to check on them, Nelda was doing most of the work and David was playing. When I brought them home, Nelda looked all beat up, face red, sweaty and tired. David ran in looking fresh and energetic. I knew who had done the work. But they divided the money evenly. That was also the only time and the only yard they mowed.

I have always enjoyed music. Wherever and whenever possible, I would be listening to music. I would sing along with the music or even dance to the music. Both my children enjoy music. We would talk about a new song and about songs we each liked. We all would find things to laugh about. There are so many funny and beautiful memories of and with my children that I have often thought about and sometimes even laugh to myself.

CHAPTER 21

ALONE AND LONELY

All this time my children were growing up, getting older, I felt myself getting lonelier, and feeling more alone. Those feelings inside of me were so much stronger now. I was not sure how to deal with them. I could not talk to Margie. I could not talk to anyone about this. At times I felt I could overcome all this and tried to encourage myself. But the courage was quickly overcome by the strong feelings I had inside.

I had what every man works so hard to have. I had a pretty wife and two wonderful children. We both worked, we were buying a house, had two cars, and lived in a quiet neighborhood. I should have been very happy.

Margie was a pretty woman who always took good care of herself. She maintained her weight proportionate to her height, dressed very nicely, was smart, and loving and caring. I know that some men wished their wives would dress up and take better care of themselves. Some of my male friends made comments about how they wished their wives would dress like Margie.

So why was I not happy? Why could I not get rid of these feelings? Why had God not answered my prayers? I tried to do everything I felt I should do so that God would see me as worthy to answer my prayers. Was he punishing me for what I had done with Old Grandfather? Maybe he would not listen to me because I had not gone to confession, but I could not bring myself to talk to a priest about that.

I started to read the Bible and went to church as often as I could. I also read books at the library on homosexuality. It was very hard for me to accept that I may be homosexual. I just knew that those feelings would go away. I had suppressed the feelings for a long time, but now they were out and very strong.

No one may really know why people are homosexual. I know that it was not by choice as some people indicate. Lord God in Heaven, I would never have chosen a life so difficult. I had already grown and lived a very difficult life being poor and working at least half of every year out in the fields. I had finally gotten to where I had a good life, even if I was still working just as many hours as I had before. Why in the world would I, or anyone else for that matter, choose a life where I would be made fun of, hated, ridiculed, called awful names, and even live in danger of being beaten up and possibly killed?

I finally got enough courage to go talk to my doctor. I made the appointment and told my doctor that I thought I might be homosexual. He gave me the name and phone number of a psychiatrist to go see. I went to see the psychiatrist.

I felt very uncomfortable when I went to see the psychiatrist. I entered the room that the psychiatrist had asked me to come into and he walked around his desk and sat down. I sat there quietly, not saying anything while he moved some papers around, maybe my file.

He asked me how he could help me. I told him I thought I was homosexual. It was very hard for me to say those words. I expected the doctor to be angry, be repulsed by me, yell at me, or anything else except, "And what seems to be the problem?" I repeated to him that I thought I was homosexual. The psychiatrist was acting as if being homosexual was not a problem. He asked me what was it about my being homosexual that I could not accept. I finally answered him and after that, I was more at ease and able to talk more freely about me and the feelings I was experiencing.

I left his office feeling very confused. I had always heard people make fun of homosexuals, say really awful things about them, and how people did not want to be around them. Now, after talking to the psychiatrist, homosexuality is something that is not all those things I had heard. I was very confused, to say the least.

I did not tell my wife or any one that I had gone to see the psychiatrist. I was not sure what to think. So I just went along as I had always done, staying busy and feeling lonely, feeling empty. I wished that I could just forget about everything and just work and enjoy my family. I wished the feelings would just go away.

But, try as I might, the feelings would not go away. I thought of all the people that would get hurt if they ever found out what I was feeling and thinking, especially Margie and our children. I could not hurt them. I did not want to hurt them.

Now, all these feelings, all this thinking I may be homosexual did not just pop up one day and I acted upon the feelings. All this trying to cope and deal with my feelings went on for years. I was tired of feeling the way I did. I was tired of feeling like I was evil for even thinking of giving in to the feelings. I feared being like Old Grandfather. I felt evil because I started thinking of just plain killing myself. I started thinking that my dying would be the best thing for all involved. My family would be better off.

During all this time of fighting the feelings I had inside, I found myself slowly sinking into depression. I was very sad inside. I wanted the feelings to go away. I wanted to be able to be a complete person inside, being happy and not being sad. I put on a good front, though. I acted happy around people.

I went to two other persons trying to find a way to get rid of my feelings. I went to a preacher of a Baptist church whom I had met before. After I told him that I felt I was homosexual, he told me to pray and that being homosexual was sinful and not to give in to the feelings. But up to now, prayer had not helped. At times I even felt angry at God. I had prayed so many times and my prayers were not answered. The feelings would not go away.

The other person I went to was a psychologist and he told me that many people were homosexual, men and women, and that I needed to accept who and what I was and try to be happy.

I dreaded having to tell my wife and my children that I was a homosexual. I did not know how I could ever hurt them in that way. I felt that everything I had worked for would be for nothing. How could I do that? But I had to do something. I was already in a severe depression. My work was the only thing I had that helped me keep my sanity. It kept me busy to where I did not have to think about me.

Parents are not always right. Parents make mistakes. Parents sometimes make bad judgments. My bad judgment at the time seemed to me to be the best way out. I will never say that what I did was okay. I know what I did was and is wrong. But I do understand when people feel like there is nothing left for them to do. And for everyone that ever feels that way, talk to someone. Talk to someone, please.

A friend of mine that I had met while I was working at the hospital had a cabin at the lake, about five miles outside of Abilene. My friend was a kind, gentle man and he and I would talk. I liked that he would listen to me talk. After I would run out of things to say, he would pray for me. He would then tell me that I was a good man and for me to always pray for God to lead my way.

I enjoyed sitting by the water and write, so he allowed me to come to his cabin on my days off during the week. Margie would be at work and the children were in school so I would go to the lake for a few hours and just relax and write.

I had become good at writing my feelings. My friend had encouraged me to write and had told me that it was good for me to do that. He said it would help me. So I would write. My friend would go the lake cabin, as he called it, only one day of the week. I stayed away from there on that day because I did not want to disturb him or bother him.

I kept on writing. I had written many times but had thrown my writings away. I told my friend that I wrote about my feelings, my thoughts and love. He told me I should save everything I wrote. It became easy for me to write what I was feeling. I remember someone once say that poems were written by depressed, slobbering drunks. I was not drunk when I was writing, but, yes, I was depressed. And so I wrote.

I was sitting by the lake watching the trees swaying in the wind. I watched how the trees would move when the wind blew, swaying to the wind and then they would stand up straight and tall when there was no wind. I also thought, that is just like me. I go along with what I am supposed to do. I have being doing just what is expected of me, what all the other men have done and are doing. They work, go to church, usually eat out after church service, help take care of the children and go home and do work at home. According to the way the men from the church talked, that is what they did. And that is what I did. No one did anything different, unusual, or exciting. They did exactly what is expected of them. And so we go along day after day, year after year doing the same thing and then we die.

If any one man changes his routine, he is seen as someone who is irresponsible, a bad person, or any other negative thing people can say about that man (or it can be a woman). It is very hard standing up and being different. A person has to be strong, or he will not endure. A tree will break if it does not bend in a strong wind.

I felt that if I admitted to what I felt, gave in to whom and what I was, I may not be able to stand the criticism, being ostracized and rebuked by my wife, children, other family members and friends. I would be alone and lost for sure.

Tree...
Sway along with the wind,
For if you stand firm,
Your strength will not endure.
I too must sway along with the crowd,
For if I should make my stand,
I have lost,
For sure.

At another time I noticed the birds flying from tree to tree. First one bird would sing then the other bird would respond. It looked like they were communicating with each other. I thought, a bird flies so freely, singing joyfully. If a bird is caged, his freedom is removed, his joy is no more.

For me, my prison was not being able to be me, not allowed to feel. I wanted to be able to let my feelings out in the open, let someone know who and what I was. I wanted to be free of all that was in my mind, all that kept going on in my head, including Old Grandfather. Because of my fear of being shunned, hated, ostracized and alone, I would be sad forever. I longed to be happy. Only through death would I be free, free to be who I am.

Just as the Sparrow treasures his freedom,
I wallow in my prison.
His joy is never ending,
My sadness forever.
And as the flutter of his wings,
I quest for my happiness.
For like the quell of the sparrow,
So is my beginning.

And so one day I felt I could not continue living this life. I hated my life at this point. I had been bad with Old Grandfather and now I had these feelings inside of me that I had desperately tried to get rid of and could not. Now I knew that I was homosexual and had finally realized that I was not able to change. I also knew that by coming out, I would hurt a lot of dear people. So what else was left for me to do?

I went to the lake cabin on a day that I knew my friend would not be there. I took a bunch of pills and lay down on the bed to go to sleep. I felt relieved. I was not afraid. And so I fell asleep.

I was awakened by some people talking, calling my name. When I opened my eyes, I saw a doctor I knew from the hospital. And my friend was there, calling for me to talk to him. I was very nauseated and felt drowsy. I called out both their names and they felt relieved. The other two people in the room were not familiar to me. The doctor and the two other persons I did not know walked to the door. My friend followed them and the doctor was talking to my friend. They left and my friend came and sat down on the bed. He told me he was very disappointed in me. I then told him everything that was going through my mind. He listened. We both talked for a long time.

It was late and I knew I had to go home. I left the cabin in my car, feeling better, still nauseated but I felt okay. I told my friend that I felt well enough to drive safely and my friend followed me home to make sure I got there safely.

That night I talked with Margie. After all I had gone through, after what I had just done, and after talking with my friend, I knew it was time. I told Margie about my feelings, about going to the psychiatrist and that I was homosexual. We both cried. But Margie was very strong, much stronger than I gave her credit for and definitely much stronger than I was. It was very hard for both of us. We decided that we would go for counseling with a priest.

The appointment was made to talk with the priest and we both went and I told the priest. The priest told us that he had counseled with men about their sexuality, and that none of those that he counseled were able to "cure" themselves of being homosexual. He then looked at my wife and told her to get a divorce and find a man who could love her and live a life as man and wife and be happy.

He then looked at me and told me to accept myself as being homosexual, to love myself and to be happy. He told me that I probably would have a difficult time ahead of me because people were not too accepting of homosexuals. He said that people did not understand homosexuality and feared homosexuality and chose to condemn the person who is homosexual. He also said that some people say they hate the sin, not the sinner, but people killed homosexuals for being homosexuals. His last words were, "May God bless you both."

Margie and I went home and sat down and talked. We both talked and cried again. She had always been a wonderful person since I had met her and she continued being that wonderful person through all the pain I had inflicted on her. I hated to have put her through all this. She did not deserve to be hurt. I wished that I had known about me before we married. Maybe I would not have hurt her as deeply.

But as I said before, even through all the pain I caused her, she continued being that remarkable woman she always had been. I told her that I was afraid I would lose my children when they found out about my being homosexual. I told her that I feared they would hate me. What Margie said to me was unbelievable. She said, "I will not let them hate you. You have been a good father to them and I will not allow them to hate you." I cried. I would always love this woman, but in a different way. I asked God to take care of her and be with her through her pain and throughout her life.

We agreed not to tell our children yet. We both felt that when the time was right, they would be told the truth. I guess all this was all too painful for us, too monstrous for us to deal with right now. We had to try to think. After at least fifteen years, our marriage was over. We did not hate each other. How could I hate this woman who was so wonderful, so loving and caring? I could never hate her. And she told me she did not hate me and I believed her. She never once was mean or ugly towards me. She never once called me a bad word or name, and believe me, there were plenty of words and names for her to call me. But she did not.

I asked her at one time if she ever suspected that I may be homosexual (and I say homosexual because back then, there was not much reference to gay). She told me that she suspected I may be homosexual because whenever anyone bad- mouthed the homosexuals, I always defended them. I took up for the homosexuals. I never realized that I was doing that.

Margie and I talked about a divorce. We both knew we would be getting a divorce. We talked about what we both wanted as far as the divorce and the children. She told me she wanted the children and I told her I wanted her to have the children. I told her I wanted her to have the house because I wanted my children to have a place to live in.

And just like that, my marriage was over. It was not that easy for me. I had to start a new life. I was still not sure about me. I was losing everything I had. It was very sad for me, but accepting myself as being homosexual was a big relief. It was now out in the open. I no longer had to hate myself. The priest had told me to love myself. It was not that easy though. I carried a lot of guilt because of how I had hurt Margie, Nelda and David.

I spent as much time as I could with my children. I missed them and needed them. I never knew what they were thinking related to my not being at home. They never asked any questions. I do not know what I would have said if they had asked. I hurt for them and for me.

I made friends with people that were homosexual like me. I started to hear people referring to homosexuals as gay. Becoming friends with these persons that were gay, I began to realize that there was a lot of hatred towards gays. I did not want people that I knew to know that I was gay. I knew that they would make it hard for me but they might also make it hard for my children. I did not want my children to be made fun of just because of me. They had already been through enough hurt. I was careful to not be obvious about my homosexuality. I did not want people knowing I was homosexual and tried to avoid people I knew, especially those from church.

I met and made new friends. I also met a man I got along with really well. We enjoyed going to the movies, visiting with other friends and watching TV. Eventually he talked about the two of us living together. I told him that it might be possible.

One day he drove me to the lake because he wanted to show me something. As we drove through a wooded part of the lake side and dusty roads, we finally entered a short driveway next to a small one story brick house. We walked into the house and I thought it was just beautiful. I asked him whose house this was and he said it was his. He said if I moved in with him, we would live here at the lake. I loved the house. It was small but he knew how to decorate houses and he had done a beautiful job.

The front door let you into the living room to the left and the kitchen to the right, all one big room. The kitchen was separated from the living room by a counter with two stool chairs on the side of the counter facing the living room. The living room had a fire place with windows on each side of the fireplace and window seats under each window. There was a step down into the next room which faced directly to the lake. There was a large picture window on the wall facing the lake and a door next to the window that opened to a large porch. That room was used as a den, with a couch, television and coffee table.

Adjoined to the den was a door that led to the bedroom. When we walked into the room, it took my breath away. The two walls facing the lake were mostly glass. You could see far to the lake from both sides. It was beautiful. There were sheer curtains on each window with drapes drawn to the sides that could be closed to provide privacy to the room. The room's main color was a light blue which was my favorite color. I had told him at one time that blue was my favorite color.

Walking out the back door to the long open space porch, I was able to see the beautiful lake. There were steps going down from the back porch to the ground level that had a walkway made of round stone steps. The steps led down the hill to a boat dock that sat a few feet into the lake waters. Next to the dock was a garage type building that had double doors opening towards the lake with rails leading from the garage into the lake. Inside the garage was a boat sitting on top of some padded rails that would electronically slide down the railed ramps and allow the boat in the water. When we were through using the boat all we had to do was steer the boat to the ramp, hook it to the ramp, turn the switch on and the ramp would slowly pull the boat into the garage, just like an elevator.

So we moved in and I started my gay life. But everyday gay life was not any different than that of straight people. We both worked, paid bills, paid child support, bought groceries and if we had money left, we would go out on the weekend. In fact we spent little time with each other. I still had to continue working my part time job or work extra at the hospital as much as I could. I spent time with my children and he spent time with his daughter and also would go help his mother.

Time goes by fast and soon five years had gone by. My partner and I did not have any money so we were not able to take nice vacations. We both seemed to be happy doing the same things day after day. My partner never complained and neither did I.

One evening while I was visiting my children in town, I receive a phone call telling me that I needed to go home immediately. I was told it was an emergency. I rushed home to the lake and I could see lights from police cars and fire trucks flashing. I parked my car and walked to the house and realized that the beautiful house we had lived in was now nothing but ashes. Only the brick walls were standing.

My partner was on one side of the yard, talking to fire officials and a policeman. The firemen were now starting to remove their equipment and load it back onto the fire truck. People that had come to see the fire were starting to leave. We had nothing left. Nothing but the clothes we had on. After every one had left, we sat there looking at the ruins and we both were numb. We could not speak.

After about what seemed like hours, we decided to go into town and rent a motel room. Very early the next morning we drove back to the lake house to sort through the ruins and hopefully find some things that we would be able to salvage. There was nothing. The fire department did not really want us to go through things until they had had time to investigate.

We contacted a close friend, DJ, and let him know what had happened. DJ owned some mobile homes and he offered to rent one of his mobile homes to us. He helped us a lot. He loaned us some kitchen supplies to help us get started towards rebuilding. The mobile home was furnished so all we needed were kitchen supplies and clothes. The whole thing seemed like a dream, a bad dream.

The fire marshal finally called and talked to us, letting us know that the investigation had been completed and it had been determined that the fire had been started by a cigarette that had been left in the ash tray. My partner and his friends had left the house to go into town to eat and someone had left a lighted cigarette in the ash tray. It was determined that the cigarette rolled off the ash tray onto the floor that had shag carpet. Sheer curtains were on the windows near the place where the cigarette had fallen on the carpet. The fire marshal stated that was the "hot spot". The house was insured but not the furniture or clothing or other belongings. And we were not able to salvage anything that we could really use. We both lost everything we owned.

But we told each other that we still had each other and we would start all over again, and so we did. We started looking for a house in town that we could rent. The mobile home was okay for now but it was not a place that we both wanted to live in for a long time. My partner found a house that he liked in a very nice part of Abilene. After talking about the house a while, he decided that he would buy the house. We both enjoyed buying things for the house and we were both happy living there.

We had lived in the new house for about a year and we were both excited about what we had done to the house. Since his work was remodeling houses and landscaping, the house was beautiful. I worked the evening shift at the hospital and also worked on the day shift whenever I was asked. As I mentioned before, I needed to work as much as I could.

Time went on and I continued to work long hours. My relationship with my partner started to deteriorate. Spending too much time at work had hurt our relationship. I had realized that I no longer wanted to be in the relationship.

Ending a relationship is not pleasant. It is painful. It takes a strong person to survive a breakup of a relationship. In my case, we had grown apart due to my being away so much. But it was still painful.

And so my first gay relationship had ended after almost six years. My ex-partner tried to talk to me, tried to get me to come back into the relationship. I thanked him for asking me to come back, but I knew it was my fault for not going on with the relationship. I told him I wanted to be on my own. He asked me for how long and I told him forever.

I continued to work at the hospital. But Old Grandfather was back. Actually, he never left. The feelings I had felt before were still there. The feelings that I had carried with me were still there to haunt me. Any time something or someone caused me pain or hurt, I believed that I deserved the pain. I believed that I deserved whatever punishment or hurt I received. What happened with Old Grandfather would always remind me that I had done something awful and I deserved to be punished for it. I knew I did not deserve to be loved because I was a bad person.

Being out of the relationship I had time to think. What was I going to do with my life? What did I want my life to be? So I decided that I would take time to think about my life and then make a decision. I made my decision.

I decided to go back to school again and work at becoming a registered nurse. I applied at Angelo State University and moved to San Angelo and started my classes. I also worked full time and more often if I could. I went for two semesters and because of finances, I had to quit again after the second semester. I guessed it was not meant for me to become a registered nurse. I moved back to Abilene.

I continued working as many hours as I could. Working was good for me. And I took time to think. My children were growing and I felt I needed to think about them. I missed them and wished I could talk to them and tell them about me. But their mother and I had both decided that they would not be told until we both felt they were ready for the truth. But I hated not being able to say anything. I know they knew something was wrong and I am sure they wanted us to tell them something. But we had made a decision to wait and that was what I was going to do. I felt very guilty. Again, parents make mistakes and I made a big one.

I also had not gotten over the bad feelings about myself and Old Grandfather. I still felt that I was evil and was going to hell. All those years of constantly being told that I would go to hell if I sinned had stuck. I still wrestled with the past. No matter what I did, how much I prayed, how hard I tried, I could not forget the past. I could not understand why I allowed Old Grandfather to do those things to me. So I kept blaming myself. I kept telling myself that it was my fault and that I had asked for it.

The one thing that I noticed since I had told Margie that I was gay and since I had accepted the fact that I was gay was that I no longer felt lonely or alone. The feelings had disappeared. I felt that I could finally be who and what I am and I accepted the fact that I was gay. I do not know what made me feel lonely or alone but now at least I did not have that to torture me. And torture it was. It is an awful feeling to feel lonely and alone.

I continued being afraid that people who Margie and I knew in Abilene would find out about my being gay. I did not want my children to be made fun of because their father was gay. I did not want them to get into fights because of me. It preyed on my mind constantly. I was constantly trying to hide my homosexuality, making sure that I did not do things or say things that would give me away. So I decided that it would be better if I moved away to another city where people did not know me and therefore my children would be protected from ridicule because of me.

I drove to Fort Worth, Texas, and applied for a job at one of the hospitals. I was told I could start working as soon as I was ready to work. It was hard deciding to move away, but I was sure that moving away was absolutely what I needed to do. So I started saving my money and preparing to move.

DJ, the friend that had offered me a place to stay after I left my ex-partner, had moved to Houston, Texas. He was working in Houston now and he would come visit his family in Abilene whenever he could. Whenever he would visit in Abilene, he would call me and we would meet at some coffee place and talk. I would tell him what little I knew that had been happening in Abilene. We would talk for a long while then I would go home and he would go back to Houston until the next time he visited Abilene.

On this particular visit to Abilene, he called me up and asked me to meet him for coffee. I met him for coffee and it was nice to get to see him and visit with him again. I told him that next time he came to visit in Abilene, I would be gone. I explained to him what I had decided to do. He then told me that he was renting a two bedroom house in Houston and that one of the bedrooms was empty. He then explained to me about the Medical Center in Houston and that I could easily get a job at any of the hospitals there. He asked me if I would move to Houston. I had never been to Houston and I told him that I would have to think about it.

I did think about it and discussed it with Margie. I basically had decided that I would make the move to Houston. My mind was already made up. I called my friend and told him I would move to Houston. And so I did.

Another bad judgment I made in moving to Houston was that I did not talk with my children about why I wanted to move. I hurt for them and as well as for myself. I just plain hurt. I was going to leave my children and I hurt. But I still felt it was the best thing for me to do. That was my way of protecting them. People can be cruel and I did not want my children getting hurt. I hope that my children can forgive me for that. But I genuinely was thinking of them in deciding to move. And I genuinely do not know why I did not talk to my children. I should have told them something. I just didn't and have felt much shame and sadness for that.

When I think about that time in my life, I still feel the pain. When I think of my son, with his longish, coal black hair, and bangs cut straight across his forehead, and when I think about my daughter, standing in the living room in front of the mirror combing her hair, I feel the pain. There are so many things I can think about of my children during their growing up years. And they are beautiful and pleasant thoughts. I still think of those times, especially when I see them all grown up with families of their own. I just love them so much.

The following are the rest of my writings that were written during the difficult times in my life. I would like to share this writings with you. Each writing has a special meaning to me.

You give me love,
Tenderness.
You believe in me,
You have faith in me.
Because of you, I have learned,
I have seen, I have known.
You are my comfort,
My fortress.

☙

Love…
Endless as the Universe
Beautiful as the Earth
And all its Nature
Such you have given me
An everlasting treasure

&

I give you this plant.
  Sunshine…
      Water…
          Food…
It grows, it blooms.
But Caution,
Too much water or sunshine,
It withers, it dies
I give you my love.
  Tenderness…
      Caring…
          Understanding…
It lives, It grows.
But be careful-
Too much of this will smother,
Too little, it dies

&

You will never know,
No, you will never know.
With time, only with time.
But if time does heal,

What will I show
You'll still be gone.
What is left to feel?
I must go on,
Yes, I must go on.
I shall not stop,
No, I must not stop.
If in time you realize,
For I am the one.
I will never know,
No, I must never know.

ଓ

Blessed be the deafening loudness of song,
For it drowns out the sound of my loneliness,
The ever-sounding cry of need.
Blessed be for dreams,
Where I live my happy life,
Fulfill my every goal.
Blessed be for distance,
For I can run away,
Escape this binding ropes of despair.
Blessed be for all the false,
That take away the truths.
Blessed be.

ଓ

Something to have, yet cannot hold.
Something to feel, yet cannot touch.
Something seen, but invisible.

Warm, yet no fire.
Radiant, but no light.
All seems impossible, yet all so real.
What comes from the Heart
Can do all these.
What comes from Love,
Brings Peace.

ରୁ

I love you.
When I say this, I am being sincere.
We have no guarantee on life and what life brings.
But we have our feelings and our lives,
And we have now.
What we feel now is all the guarantee we need.
It may not last, but if we live our lives
For what might happen tomorrow,
We will not enjoy today.
We laugh, We cry, We feel, We share.
We enjoy what we have now,
A unique experience.
If we look for a guarantee to life
And life's happenings,
We are by-passed.
We have lost.

ରୁ

You need not feel alone,
For when not in your presence,
My thoughts are of you.

Remembering your gentleness,
Your warm brown eyes,
Your radiant smile.
You need not be alone,
For whenever in need,
Whatever the want,
I will be there.
Always be there.

ও

So we give each other space...
The space to think,
The space to be,
The space to cover up,
The things we dare not face.
With pride we say, this is what I need.
Oh foolish hearts...
So blind you cannot see.
For space is only emptiness and lonliness,
Of Love that was meant to be.

ও

Lie there and sleep, My Love.
Lie there and sleep.
Enjoy the dreams we long to keep,
That bring such comfort, such peace.
And as I watch you sleep,
I feel a warmth, a love so deep,
That special feeling, so hard to find.
For you are so gentle, so kind.

You have changed my life in every way.
I treasure each moment of every day.
So do not awaken yet, this day so new,
That I may watch you sleep, my eyes fill of you.
I leave you now, for I must go…
But you go with me, my heart aglow.
 While you lie there and sleep, my love,
Lie there and sleep.

ॐ

Why?
What I can give,
You would never be able to find.
Can't you see?
Oh, why can't you see?
It's so plain, so simple.
Take it, don't look beyond.
Don't seek.
Why?
But can't you see?
If you pass it by,
 Oh, but if you pass it by,
 I may not be here,
And you'll wonder,
Why?

ॐ

I reach out to emptiness,
For you are not there.
Your big brown eyes,

Laughter that fills life around you.
The warmth of your touch,
The richness I feel when you say….
Only the dreams,
The memories.
For all is gone,
All past,
And I feel….
The emptiness.

ભ

Thank you for a wonderful weekend.
It is a chapter in my life I will always remember.
Christmas came early to me this year,
And you made it all possible.
For some of us, little things are worth more than money can
buy.
You gave, I took.
I gave, You took.
A beautiful experience.
When tomorrow comes, we go on with our lives as before.
But it did happen to me,
And I felt it.
As beautiful, if not more beautiful than life itself.
And its mine,
To hold,
To treasure.
A beautiful Christmas.

ભ

Colorfull flowers
Beautiful stems,
Different size buttons,
Held by a vase.
Just as tenderness,
Caring,
And Love,
Are held by a Heart.

CHAPTER 22

HOUSTON 1980

I moved to Houston the first weekend of March of 1980. I drove my old 1974 Ford Torino following a medium sized U-Haul truck with furniture that my friend was moving to Houston. I followed him all the way from Abilene, stopping only for gas and to eat.

I had lived in Melvin with a population of six hundred plus people and then in Abilene with a population of ninety thousand people. I thought Abilene was big. When we got to Houston I panicked. Cars everywhere and huge buildings like those on television or the movies. I felt lost in such a huge city, but yet, excited about making a change. It was beautiful, but at the same time very scary. Here I was a thirty two year old man and scared of being in a large city. Wow, it was different.

I had only brought my clothes, my toiletries and two quilts that my mother had hand sown for me and one pillow. Darrell had told me that the extra bedroom was empty and that is how it was. Empty. It was hardwood floor with a closet and four windows, two windows on each side of the corner of the outer walls.

I told myself I did not mind sleeping on the hardwood floor, that this was the beginning of a new life for me. When I woke up the next morning after my first night of sleeping on the floor, I was not too sure I was going to enjoy this new beginning. I hurt all over. I was supposed to be in shape because of all the jogging I did and all kinds of calisthenics. I was in pain. The only parts of my body that were not in pain were the soles of my feet and the top of my head. Every part in-between was in pain. But I told myself, after the first two nights, I would get used to it and I would be okay.

I went to the medical center to find a job. I had never seen so many hospitals and so many medical personnel in my life. Darrell was right, Houston did have one of the largest medical centers in the world. After applying for a job and finding a job right away, I spent the rest of the day at the medical center sightseeing and the area that is called Montrose.

I was told by Darrell that we lived in the middle of the gay area of Houston. And I had never seen so many gays in my life. Some were friendly and some not so friendly. The Montrose area was big and there was so much to see. Houston had so much for me to see and so much for me to learn. One thing I did pay attention to was the warning that I should not be out at night alone. And I never did walk alone after dark.

I was so intrigued by the tall buildings downtown. I had not been downtown yet but just seeing the buildings from a few blocks from the house was so interesting. Wow! I was in Houston.

And I was still sleeping on the floor. It had gotten a little bit better. I got a large cardboard box that I flattened out and used as my mattress. It helped ease the hardness of the hardwood floor and allowed my body to get over the pain. I had to work for a while before I could think about buying a bed. I had no money. What little money I had brought with me, I had to save for gas and lunch for work. I had gotten another large cardboard box that I turned upside down and used as a dresser.

For the first two weeks of living in Houston, I worked, came home and stayed home. I did not attempt to go out with my friend because I did not have the money to go out and I did not really like going places without money. So I stayed home.

Right before the last week of March, after coming home from work, Darrell told me that a friend of his would be coming by to pick him up to go eat. Darrell told me that I could come along with them. I thanked him for the invite but I told him I would be going to bed early and maybe some other time.

Darrell was not too happy that I had declined the invitation. When he would become upset with me he would always call me Joseph instead of Joe. And he did say, "Joseph, you need to get out more. You have stayed home since you moved here from Abilene." I needed time to get adjusted to being in a new place and new surroundings and I also needed the money to go out.

I was sitting on the sofa in the living room watching TV when Darrell's friend came by. I was introduced to the friend and immediately wished I had said yes on going out to eat with them. The "friend" was handsome and nice and handsome and friendly and handsome and handsome some more. The friend and I visited while he waited for Darrell to be ready. We had a very nice visit. When they left, the new friend stated that maybe we could visit some more if I was still awake. I knew I could easily remember his name. Yes, you guessed it. His name was David.

I went to bed with my clothes on knowing that I would make sure I was awake when Darrell and David came home. I wanted to visit with the new friend. I fell asleep.

I had to wake up early to go work, even though it was Saturday. I went to work and very often during the day I thought about the new friend. I wished I could see him again. But then I thought that I was not someone he would be interested in, especially if he found out I slept on the floor. It saddened me as I told myself to forget about him.

I got off work and drove home thinking of going walking and then relaxing before I went to bed early again. Medical personnel have to work on weekends and I was used to it. Having a day or two off during the week was convenient for me so I could do those things that some people cannot get done on weekends.

I parked my car on the street in front of the house and walked in. Darrell was sitting on the sofa reading a book. He was a teacher and he enjoyed reading. He put his book down as he looked at me and asked how my day had gone. I said fine as I walked past him to my bedroom. I opened the door to my bedroom and stood there in the doorway. There was an old canvass army cot and my quilts were placed on the cot and the pillow on one end of the cot. Darrell had walked behind me and was standing there smiling.

I asked him who had brought the cot and spread the quilts and placed the pillow on the end of the cot. He smiled and said David. He then explained that while they ate, the new friend had asked him questions about me and in the process, Darrell had told him I was sleeping on the floor. David had felt bad about it and had brought the cot, set it up and placed the quilts and pillow on top. "And by the way," Darrell said "David is coming over this evening to visit with us."

I told Darrell that I had enjoyed visiting with David and he said that David had apparently enjoyed the visit also. I was excited. I liked the idea of having a chance to thank him for the caring gesture but also to hopefully get to know him better. And so my new friend arrived.

Darrell, David and I visited for several hours. I thanked him for bringing the cot for me to use. He explained that he had remembered about the cot that had been in storage for a very long time. I let him know how much I appreciated him doing that and I would take good care of the cot. He laughed and said that it really was old and he hoped that the canvas did not tear up and me fall through to the floor. We all laughed about it but I was glad to have the cot. David stated he had to leave because he had to work the next day, but he told us he enjoyed the visit and he hoped to see us again.

It was on a Wednesday, three days after David had come to visit, when I heard from him again. Darrell had entered the hospital for a planned surgical procedure on the Tuesday after the visit. On Wednesday, David called to check on Darrell. David and I started to see each other quite frequently after that Wednesday call.

Darrell got out of the hospital and came home to recuperate from the surgery. I continued working at the Medical

Center. David and I did not go out much but we spent a lot of time talking with each other and also visiting with Darrell and some other friends.

David was different from other men. He was extremely intelligent. I enjoyed talking with him because he usually always brought up a new word that I may not have heard before and it would become a learning experience for me. David seemed to enjoy teaching me and helping me to learn. We laughed a lot. He had a good sense of humor. We learned about each other's likes and dislikes, and I learned a lot about David. I would be foolish to say that I liked everything about him, but there were some things I was not sure I liked about him, some things that I learned to like about him, and then the things that I will forever be thankful that I learned from him.

I quickly learned that David did not like to spend money. He did not enjoy going out to eat at places he felt were expensive. Since I did not have the money to spend at expensive places, I was happy to eat at places he chose. I had grown up poor all my life and had never eaten in an expensive place. The important thing was that we were both happy eating where ever we ate.

I worked a lot of extra hours because I needed the money to send to my children and to be able to help Darrell with the rent, groceries, and utilities. Spending time with each other was sometimes very limited, but David seemed to understand and encouraged me to work whatever amount of time I needed to work. I always looked forward to whatever small amount of time I could spend with him.

As time went on, our feelings for each other grew. The one thing I noticed about David was that he always showed so much concern about me. He kept mentioning the cot that I slept on. He felt that I needed a bed and I felt and told him the cot was good enough for now. He always wanted to know if I had enough food to eat, enough money for gas, enough rest so that I would not get sick from working so much. He was always wanting to make me more comfortable, such as placing pillows behind my back or my head so I could be more comfortable, wanting me to take my shoes off to rest my feet since I walked all day at work and so many other little things.

David and my relationship went on until the end of May. Darrell had informed me that he had been offered a job where he would get the opportunity to teach overseas and he had accepted. Before he went to India to teach, he would have to go to El Paso for training. Darrell asked me if I would move to El Paso with him. He felt that he enjoyed our friendship and since I was a nurse, I could easily get a job there. I hated for Darrell to move away, but I knew that I could not move away from Houston. I had learned to like Houston and besides, David was here and I did not want to leave him.

That evening David came to pick me up to go eat. I informed him that I needed to find an apartment and I told him why. He let me know that he would help me find an apartment. We both decided that I wanted an apartment in the Montrose area. So we looked at apartments but there were no apartments available in the places we went to and some were too expensive for me. The ones that were available, we both felt, were not in such good neighborhoods.

Because I had to work long hours, I did not have much time to look for an apartment. Very soon I had to worry about Darrell moving to El Paso and that I must find an apartment. Because time had basically run out, David invited me to move in with him until I found an apartment. I felt that I really did not want to move in with him since we had only known each other a few months and I told him so. David insisted I move in and said he could help me look for an apartment without having to rush. And so in July 1980, I moved in with David and Darrell moved on to El Paso.

David owned a two-story brick home in the Montrose area. The two-story home had been remodeled and made into upstairs and downstairs apartments. David lived in the upstairs part of his home and the downstairs apartment was leased out to a middle-aged male couple. The house was just a few minutes from the medical center where I worked. It also was close to the university where I would go walking in the evenings on the days that I would get off work early and on weekends when I was off work.

We did look for an apartment for me on the weekends that I was off but David would make all kinds of excuses for me not to get the apartment that I felt was good for me. Each time we found an apartment that I found interesting, he would say that I could think about the apartment while we ate. And we would go eat. After we ate, we would go home and I would not see about the apartment. Eventually he told me he wanted me to stay with him.

David and I were as different as day and night. He and I would spend hours talking and telling each other about our childhood, our teenage years, going through school, working and living our lives up until we met. We had very different backgrounds. When I would tell him about how I grew up he would sometimes cry. Sometimes we would both cry. The one thing I could not bring myself to tell him was about Old Grandfather and the feelings of my being ugly, worthless, and responsible for everything that had happened to me. These feelings were still with me. If I stayed busy with work I did not have to think about that.

David was a very different person from most people I had known. He was very precise and methodical. He showed me exactly how he wanted things done and I did exactly as he told me. As I got to know him better I started to see a side of him that I began to like and appreciate. I do not think too many people knew that side of David that I got to know. At first, he seemed hard and critical or honest to the point that he would hurt my feelings and seemed cruel. He was very direct in what he said and I learned that he really meant well and he did not mean to hurt my feelings.

An example of what I am talking about: David used to correct me when I mispronounced a word. Because I am Hispanic and English is my second language, I knew that I did mispronounce words. When he would correct me, I felt he cared and wanted me to learn to speak correctly. But the way he corrected me on mispronounced words and the reason he gave as to why he helped me pronounce them correctly was stern but kind at the same time, if that makes any sense. He told me I needed to learn to pronounce words correctly because I turned people off by sounding uneducated. If you wonder why I did not get upset, I wanted to learn to pronounce words correctly. I knew that I mispronounced words. I had been made fun of before. So I received his correcting me with appreciation.

A good example of how I mispronounce words or sounds of vowels is the following: I was at a party and was talking with a preacher, his wife, and about three other church members. The preacher asked me about a street name related to the topic we were discussing. The street name is

Beechnut, but I gave it a "bitchnut" pronunciation. The preacher smiled and I continued my story but noticed that every time I said "bitchnut", they all would smile. I came home, told David what had happened, and he laughed and explained why. I was not aware I was doing that.

Another David example: After living with David for about a year, he learned about all the responsibilities I had concerning my children and also helping my parents. He told me he resented my family because if I did not have to help them financially, I would have very good money. I did not respond to that but I thought to myself, "so do I, sometimes."

Still another David example: Our first Christmas together, I wanted to give him something as a Christmas gift. I had no idea what to get him for his gift. I got him a key chain with his initials and wrapped it and gave it to him. He did not even bother to open the gift. He was washing dishes and told me to take it back and get my money back. He said he really did not need anything. I kept the key chain for myself.

But, in living with David, I also began to know him much better. I got to know the full extent of his kindness, and the loving and caring person that he was. There were things that I began to see in him that made me feel a very strong love for him. If we were going into or coming out of an eating establishment and a homeless person would ask for money, David would tell them that he would not give them any money. But he would also tell them that if they were hungry, he would buy them something to eat. And very often they would accept. David would tell me not to give them money because they might not use it for food. David would tell me to offer to buy them food if I wanted to do that.

One Saturday we were walking into the grocery store. There was a woman with a little baby that was about one to two years old. The woman asked if we could spare money for milk for her little girl. I said no but David said yes as he took out a five dollar bill and gave it to the lady. Inside the store he asked me why I would not give her any money to buy milk for the baby and I told him that the woman was wearing earrings, lots of makeup, several rings on her fingers, a nice dress and nice shoes. I said that if she could afford all that, she could buy the baby some milk. David said that maybe I was right but maybe not, but that if the woman was trying to get money for herself instead of the baby, she would have to answer for that.

I continued to work long hours and David was constantly concerned that I got enough rest while I was at home. In the mornings, he would get up and tried to fix breakfast for me to eat before I went to work. Because I am not much of a breakfast eater, I usually carried a snack to work. David also did the laundry for me. Actually that was because he told me he did not want me touching his washer and dryer. I did not like him doing the laundry for me but he would get my dirty clothes and wash them while I was at work. He told me that he had to do his own laundry anyway, so it was not a problem doing my laundry with his.

I noticed that David would frequently tell me to call my parents. He would frequently ask me if I had talked to my Mother. He would also push for me to go visit my Mother whenever I had a weekend off. He would offer to go with me when I would tell him that it was a very long drive and I would get tired. So we would make the long trip to see my parents. I always did what he told me to do.

One time I asked David why he was always asking me if I had called my Mother or wanting me to visit my Mother. He told me that his mother had been sick and that he should have gone to see her instead of going to work on the weekends. He told me that he should have gone to see his mother and that he would always regret not going to see her. He would cry every time he thought about that. He would tell me that I should do things for my parents while they were alive and if I did, I would never feel regret or bad after they were gone. And so I did what he told me to do.

David also showed me how to save money. He was always telling me I needed to save money. And I did what he told me to do to save money. On my payday, he and I would go to the bank and he would tell me how much to save, spend, pay, etc. If he felt I was making a mistake, he would tell me his opinion.

I also noticed something very peculiar about David. Every time we were getting ready to go somewhere, it would take a while for him to do a certain ritual. He would check the three locks on the back door, check the stove burners by touching each one, and then check the thermostat. Then he would go back and recheck the back door locks, touch the stove burners and recheck the thermostat. And he would do this a third time. Then he would be ready to go. If he did not do his little ritual three times, no matter how far from the house we would be, we had to turn back and come home so he could check the back door, the stove and the thermostat.

Many years later, he and I saw the movie with Jack Nicholson, *As Good As It Gets.* During the movie, I noticed that he would cry during certain parts of the movie. After we left the theater and were on our way home, he asked,

"Did you see me in that movie?" I looked at him and he got teary eyed. He said, "That was me. I do the same thing." He asked me if he had said hurting things to me like the character in the movie. I nodded yes. He then told me that he knew that people did not like him because he would say exactly what he thought. He said he did not mean to hurt anyone. I told him I understood.

David maintained the small yard landscape very nicely and meticulously. He spent weekends working on the yard and then washed his car. When he worked on his yard, he did everything very routinely, and exact. He usually started early in the morning and worked all day trimming and mowing and watering the yard. When trimming the yard, he would use a two-by-four board about two to three feet long to edge in a straight line. He would get a knife and edge around the flower beds using the knife and board. He would get down on his knees and used a foam pad to protect his knees.

I frequently offered to help David work in the yard, but he would always say no and would tell me to go rest. Sometimes he would have me pick up after he was through.

David had a tenant that was a close friend of his who lived in the garage apartment. His friend had been living in the garage apartment for several years. His friend was not too friendly towards me when I first moved in with David. I was later told that it was because his friend was afraid I would only stay long enough to learn the premises and later move out and come and steal from them. For me, it was okay for his friend not to trust me because David trusted me and I was happy.

David's friend started to develop health problems. He had told David that his grandfather had died at age fifty-five, his father had died at age fifty-five and that he too would die at age fifty-five. David talked his friend into going to see different doctors for their opinions and they mostly each gave a different diagnosis. So we really did not know for sure what his health problem was. I know I took him to at least two doctors that would run the same tests each time and give different opinions.

David's friend was getting worse and he wanted to go to Austin to see his mother who was in a nursing home with dementia. I drove David's friend to Austin so he could get to see his mother. It was a very sad situation. His mother did not even know who he was and it was very hard on David's friend. I felt very sorry for him.

Shortly thereafter, David's friend went into the hospital, went into a coma and died. He was fifty-five years old. He was cremated and David brought the ashes to his house because he had made a promise to his friend to spread his ashes in the Grand Canyon.

David and I still loved and cared for each other very much but our relationship had become more as very good friends. I was working most of the time, especially on weekends when David was home. Slowly we began to realize that our relationship was more as two friends that lived as roommates and not a love relationship. We still went to the grocery stores, out to eat, to exercise at the gym we had joined, to the movies, and to visit with friends as we used to do.

After his friend died, I told David I wanted to move into the garage apartment. We sat down and discussed our relationship. It had been a little over a year now. We both knew we loved each other, but I wanted a place of my own. David used to say we were co-dependent on each other. I do not know if he was right but we seemed to enjoy each other's company. And so I moved into the garage apartment.

David seemed to have as much enjoyment helping me decorate the apartment as I did. He spent more time in my apartment than he did in his. It was fine with me because he was an important part of my life. I really enjoyed having my own place though. It was my apartment and I could live here as I pleased.

I thoroughly enjoyed living in the garage apartment. David would come by every day and we would eat and watch television. I worked long hours but I was very happy. Or so I thought. When I was alone Old Grandfather kept coming back. I felt dirty, ugly, not worth anything and I would get depressed.

David would notice when I would get into my depressive moods. He would ask me what was wrong and wondered if I was sick from too much work. He would tell me to take a few days off. Finally one day I told David a little bit about Old Grandfather. I told him how I felt that no one could love me and about feeling worthless and ugly. David told me he felt really bad about everything that happened to me, but that he did not agree with me that I deserved to be treated badly. He asked me if I had gone to a therapist to help me. I told him I had only gone to the psychiatrist due to my homosexuality, but not about Old Grandfather.

Strangely enough, one day we were watching the Oprah Winfry show. The show was about sexually abused children. The part that stuck with me was where Oprah said that the child is not to blame for being sexually abused. Her statement was, "How can a five or six year old know what is going on? What would they know at that age? A child is not to blame for him or her being sexually abused."

I started to cry. The more I thought about what Oprah said, the more I thought of what happened to me. What had I done to cause Old Grandfather to do that to me? I could not think of anything that I might have done or said that made him do that to me. I had just enjoyed the animals. I enjoyed feeding the chickens. I enjoyed gathering the eggs. What had I done? Why did he do that to me?

David helped me find a psychologist and I went. I did not know what to expect by going to the psychologist. I did not know if I could go more than once to the psychologist. Eighty-five dollars an hour was not chicken feed. David told me to go one time and see how I felt about the psychologist.

The psychologist was a very nice lady who made me feel comfortable right from the start. She asked me a few questions about myself having to do with the present. Then she told me to tell her about my past, to tell her as much as I could or as much as I wanted to. She helped me get started by asking one or two questions about the surroundings, the animals, and feeding the animals. Then I talked. I told as much as I could in one hour. When the hour was up, she told me that she wanted for me to come back in one week. I agreed.

When I left her office, I felt light on my feet. I felt relieved. This was the first time I had really talked to anyone about Old Grandfather. No one knew about Old Grandfather and me except David, whom I had told a small part of what happened. The psychologist had not been repulsed by what I had told her. I had been able to talk about Old Grandfather and I felt good. I decided I wanted to go back the next week.

David was waiting in my garage apartment when I got home. He asked how the meeting had gone. I sat down and realized that I felt very relaxed, at ease. I told him how "light" I felt, that I had been able to talk about Old Grandfather and that I was going back next week. David agreed that I should go back.

It was next week now and I went to the psychologist again. We talked again, but with me doing most of the talking. I kept going back every week until the psychologist and I felt that I did not have to come back to see her. My meetings with her were done, but I still had a lot of work to do for myself, with myself. There were some things that we were not able to "break through" as she phrased it, but she felt that maybe I could someday do that on my own or with the help of someone.

Through the meetings with the psychologist I learned to accept that what Old Grandfather did to me was not my fault. I did not cause any of that to happen to me. The blame is on Old Grandfather. He did something that he should not have done and had caused me to believe that I was to blame. Old Grandfather made me believe that I would be punished and I believed it because I was a child.

To blame myself and to tell myself that I did not deserve to be loved was part of what I learned to believe because of the frequent instruction from the church about sinning and going to hell. I kept "beating" myself mentally as I kept blaming myself. For the terrible things that happened to me, I should have been comforted, held, made to feel safe, but my parents did not know what had happened to me.

The whole thing became a vicious cycle in me and it tortured me for many years. My not talking to or confiding in someone made it harder on me. I carried a huge bag full of quilt for many years, and it never was my fault. It was very hard for me to believe that it was not my fault and it was rather hard to let it sink in.

I kept thinking to myself that it had not been my fault and that I had not been as bad as I had believed myself to be. I cried many times just thinking about that. *It was not my fault.* Why would any man want to do that to a child? To a child, mind you. I did not feel any anger or hatred towards Old Grandfather. I do not remember ever feeling hatred or anger towards Old Grandfather. All I remember is fear. I would have to stop the fear. I told myself that I would not let Old Grandfather control me any longer. I would not give him the time of day.

But it was not as easy as it may sound. I found out that I could not just say that I would not let Old Grandfather control me any longer. He did, for a long time. And sometimes, he still tries to. Most importantly, I was able to talk about what happened to me. I can now talk about what happened to me and not feel ashamed, not feel that I had done a terrible, sinful thing and that I am going to hell for it.

Now I can talk about what happened to me and I do not mind talking about it. If I can help one person, one child by talking about my ordeal, then I will keep on talking about it. And I will never understand how any one that has gone through what I have gone through, could do that same horrific thing to some other child. I would never want any one, especially children, to go through what I went through.

One time I went to eat with a large group of people from a church that I used to attend for a while. The church group was very nice and to this day, I still consider several of them my friends. Among the group was a priest. Somehow the conversation about child molesters arose. The priest said that child molesters should be rehabilitated. Someone else mentioned the cost to rehabilitate child molesters and that we would end up paying. Someone else said that rehabilitation for child molesters does not work.

I became angry. Just the thought of rehabilitating child molesters angered me. I asked about the victims. Who helps the victims? It cost me eighty-five dollars an hour to be able to deal with what a child molester did to me. No one was there to help pay for the sessions due to what someone else did to me.

I went on to say that a child molester ruins a child's life, puts a child through hell and no one offers to pay for rehabilitating the child. I said a person that has been sexually abused never forgets. We may learn to live with it, but we never forget. Some other person in the group said the child molester should get the electric chair. I said certainly not. They all looked at me, puzzled because of how I had talked about the child molester. I said not an electric chair. It should be a couch, and electrocute three or four at one time. The priest got up and left. Maybe I said too much.

I thought about the time when my son was growing up and how I felt that I needed to protect him. I never told anyone about the fear I felt thinking if something like that should happen to my son. I felt I could kill any person that touched my son in that way. I am not a violent person, but I feel anger when I hear of some person sexually abusing a child. And I do not hear about the child that got abused, what is done to help that child. I have heard people talk about the abuser, about treatment for the abuser, but never about the abused.

I suffered for many years for what Old Grandfather did to me, I never will forget what he did to me, and may never fully be rid of him in my life. I think of what a child will go through for the rest of his life if that happens to him or her. My heart aches for them.

I think of that little boy being molested by Old Grandfather. I think of the fear, the hundreds of times that he died inside for what happened to him, the anguish, the guilt and the pain he went through for all those years. I wish I could hold that little boy, tell him that everything is fine. I want to take his pain away, his fears and tell him that no one will ever hurt him again. I want to protect him, hold him and make him feel safe. Oh, how I wish I could do that. How that little boy needed that. How that little boy still needs that. It never goes away.

Maybe I will never get completely over some of those feelings but I feel so much better inside. I keep telling myself that I am worthy of being loved, of being just as good as the next person.

As I have said, David and I talked about our past on several occasions. He would tell me about himself and when he was growing up. I know one thing, he loved his family. He talked very fondly about his mother. Many times he would cry while telling me the things about his mother that made him happy to think about. Like the time his mother came to stay with him in Houston and she taught his little Chihuahua to climb the stairs.

He frequently talked about his older brother and many times said he wished he could have been close to him. He made a couple of calls to his older brother, but I know he wished he could have been able to call him more often.

David spoke about his sister and I could tell he loved his sister. He was proud of her, her accomplishments, and would tell me stories about him and his sister when they were growing up. He would laugh about some of the things that happened. I would laugh with him also. I felt so much joy in hearing him laugh.

And then there were the stories about his little brother. He would laugh about some of the things that he said happened with his little brother. David would always talk about and was very proud of his little brother's children. It gave him great pleasure to go to the school reunions and if he got to see his little brother's children, he would talk for days about them. I say children, but they, a son and a daughter, were really grown, married and with children. David had told me that if anything ever happened to him, that I should call his little brother's son before calling anyone else.

Many years went by, and they went by fast. David and I would do many things together. Going to the movies was good with us. I had some friends that sometimes would invite me to their parties, dinners or whatever they were having, and David would go with me.

And boy, David enjoyed going to any sale that the grocery stores were having. Sometimes we would drive to at least four or five grocery stores just to buy three to five items that were on sale. I reminded him about the gas he spent driving to all those places and he would say he knew that he may be spending more money on gas than what he saved on the sales. He would say that buying something on sale gave him great pleasure. So we drove to all those places and sometimes all the way to Pasadena, Texas. We would both laugh about it but we had fun.

I was sending child support payments to my children so I still had to work lots of hours. Because many times I worked double shifts, I did not have much time to take care of the bills and banking. So David offered to do that for me. He said he did not mind doing that for me, since he had to pay his bills and go to the bank. So he started taking over my bills and banking and all I would do was sign the checks.

David was a person I could trust and I trusted him completely. Never, ever did I feel that I could not trust David. If he borrowed one penny from me, he would pay it back. And I am not exaggerating, but at the same time, if I owed him a penny, he would expect for me to pay him that penny back. When I would say to him that it was only a penny, he would say, "A penny is a penny."

The years continued to go by and the love and friendship that David and I had grew stronger. I would ask for his opinion on my finances and he would give me his opinion. He seemed to enjoy helping me learn, especially related to money. If he felt an item I wanted was too expensive, he would explain to me why the item was not worth the money or how I could do without the item and save my money.

But the most difficult subject he had teaching me was math. I hate math. He used to tell me I did not hate math. He kept telling me that once I learned math, I would know that it was not as bad as I thought.

So David taught me math. He would always start with a pie, cutting the pie into so many pieces. He taught me fractions and percentages. Because of the difficulty I had learning fractions and because every teaching session started with cutting a pie into small pieces, it got to where I could not stand to hear about pies. I would teasingly ask him if we could use a cake instead. But he never gave up. Every chance he had, he would teach me math. He taught me easy ways to figure out a percentage on items at the stores that were selling at a certain percent off. We would go through the store with him picking up an item and asking what the price of the item would be when I would subtract the percentage discount. If I got the correct sale price of the item after deducting the discount, he would praise me and tell me how good I was doing.

I would get tired trying to learn fractions way before he ever got tired of teaching me. In fact, David never did get tired of trying to teach me. I did learn some things but like I have said, math is very complicated and just when I think I understand it, I don't. If my co-workers or friends ask me to help them out on fractions or anything having to do with math, I will tell them, "One plus one is three. Anything else you want to know?" They will leave me alone.

Now when it comes to nursing math, I know it well and can figure out dosages and it comes easy to me. I feel that the nursing math is different from regular math. I don't know if that is true, but I am good at the nursing math. I have to be. As a registered nurse, I cannot afford to make mistakes figuring out dosages.

David encouraged me on anything I felt I could not do, on anything that I needed to do, or anything that I wanted to do. He would encourage me and would tell me to keep on trying until I accomplished whatever it was I wanted or needed to accomplish. David would not let me give up. When I told him about the two attempts of trying to complete my studies to become a registered nurse, he told me I had to go back to school and get my registered nurse license. I did not feel that I could complete my studies and I would have to drop out again, just as I had to do the other two times.

One weekend I went to visit my children in Abilene after a couple of years of living in Houston. I enjoyed the trip. I enjoyed seeing my children. When I got back from Abilene, I called David to come over to my garage apartment. When he came in I showed him to the dining table where I had a stack of envelopes. He asked me what that was, I told him all those were bills I owed on and was behind on. Margie had given me a stack of bills that needed to have been paid months ago. She told me that she did not have money to pay those bills.

David went through the stack of bills and sorted them out by company or place where I owed. When he was finished sorting the bills he said, you are going to pay those bills and you can do it. I sat there as he explained to me how I would pay those bills. He told me that I would call each place I owed money to, explain to them that I would pay those bills, and give them my new phone number and address. I did what he told me to do.

I called each business I owed money to and informed them that I was going to pay the bill. Some of the places were agreeable, some did not seem to get their hopes up about getting paid, and some were downright rude and ugly. I would listen to what they had to say and then repeat to them that I would pay what I owed them.

David then told me that I would send the minimal amount payment on each bill. If I could, I would send the smallest bill an extra payment. After I paid off the smallest bill, I would then add the amount that I had paid monthly on the small bill and add it to the next smallest bill. After I paid the next to the smallest bill, I would add the amount of those two to the next bill and so on until I paid all the bills.

Since I was registered with a nursing agency that would find employment for me, I called the agency. I told them I was checking to see if they had any work for me. The agency would send me to work at hospitals, but private duty cases always came up and I did not mind doing private duty. I was told that I had called just at the right time. They had a private duty case for me. So I accepted this case, not knowing what I was getting into. Both David and I were excited because I could pay off my bills more quickly.

The case I was assigned to was providing care to a prince. I went to the unit where I was instructed to go and the nurse at the nurses' station directed me to the room. A nurse coming off the night shift came out of the room and we went to the nurses' lounge where I would get my report before I went to take care of the patient.

Every morning I would get to the hospital at six thirty a.m. and get a report from the outgoing nurse, so that I could start work at seven. The outgoing nurse would cry while giving the report. She would cry because of the way she was treated by the prince and his entourage. Along with the prince was his personal physician from the country the prince was from, the prince's brother, a general, and two other men that I did not know who or what they were. There were also two other men that I took as being his workers or slaves since they were treated poorly.

Since he was a prince, he was expected to be treated like a prince. I did not know that they treated nurses like s_ _ t and I did not know that I would have my first experience with migraine headaches. I worked twelve hour shifts, seven a.m. to seven p.m. and off on Sundays. I hated my job.

I guess I would say that I am the only person alive that has dropped a prince on the floor and has lived to talk about it. I assisted the prince to the bathroom and stood outside the bathroom door and tried to guess when he was ready for me to help him. He was paralyzed on one side, both arm and leg. The prince spoke no English, none, nada, zilch and I did not speak his language. I asked through the door if he was ready and there was no answer. He never made a sound. I open the door slightly to see if he was alright. When I looked in the bathroom, he was leaning to one side holding on with his good arm. I rushed in to help and because he was leaning so low I could not lift him up. I gently and slowly eased him to the floor so that I could get a better hold on him and lift him up. After I got him ready for the day, his entourage started coming in.

The first one who came in was his personal physician. Immediately the prince started talking to the physician. I knew the prince was telling him what had happened because during the conversation with his physician, the prince would look at me and make faces at me and would say what sounded like "batha" to me. The physician then asked me what happened and I explained to him what had happened. The physician then told me that I should be there at the ready for whatever the prince needed. I told the physician that I tried to be there but that the prince did not want me in the bathroom when he was sitting on the commode and would not call me when he was ready for me to help him. The physician informed me that I was there to wait on the prince, the prince was not there to wait for me.

As the rest of the entourage kept coming in to see the prince, the prince would repeat the same thing to each person and then each person would then look at me and then "batha" towards me. I knew that it must not be something good or nice that they said to me. I would just sit there and look at each one of them as they would each "batha" me. As I looked at each one of them I would think about the money and the bills I needed to pay off. The "batha" was not so bad.

At the end of my shift, after twelve awful hours, the night nurse would come in and I would give her a report. The nurse and I shared reasons why we both hated taking care of the prince. The nurse told me she wanted to quit but her husband had told her that it was good money and that he would physically get her dressed and drag her here himself if she did not go work.

Besides the problem with communication, there was another big problem. The prince thought I was his slave. The prince would be taken out to eat outside of the hospital. They drove him in a limousine and I had to come along to push the wheelchair. I was not allowed to eat while they ate. I had to wait with the limousine driver until they got through eating. After we got back to the hospital and had taken the prince back to his room, then I was allowed to go eat. This would be about two or three p.m.

On several occasions, one of the men from his entourage would come and get me before I could get through eating. When I tried to explain that I was not through eating, the man would tell me to come back now, the prince needed me. And when I got there, it was usually for something like tying his shoe string, or helping him change his shirt, as he changed two or three times a day, or helping transfer him to the wheelchair or from the wheelchair. Whatever the reason, I was not allowed to finish my lunch.

From the first day that I started taking care of the prince, I would be deathly ill with a migraine headache by the end of each day. And because of the headaches, I could not drive myself home. David would drop me off at work in the mornings and pick me up from work in the evenings.

When David would come to pick me up from work I would be so sick that I would open the back door of his car, get in and lie down on the back seat of the car until I got home. I would rush up the stairs into the apartment, rush to the bed and lie down, shoes and all. David would come into the apartment, take my shoes off my feet, cover me up and leave. Every morning I would wake up and take a few minutes to see if I was sick. Oh, how I wished I was sick so I did not have to go work. I wanted to quit that case so badly, but I kept thinking of those bills.

The patient and his entourage did not have any respect for people and especially not for women. Example: When we would take the patient downstairs for physical therapy, we would all go to the elevator. People would be waiting at the elevator when we would get there. Some of the men in his entourage would walk to the elevator, and walk in front of the people already standing there waiting. When the elevator would arrive, the men would block the people from getting on the elevator while I rolled the wheelchair into the elevator. Then all the men in his entourage would follow into the elevator and the elevator would be full. They would push the button to close the elevator doors and no one else could get in.

Well, finally the day came when David informed me that I had only one more payment to make and all my bills would be paid off. On the last week before the last payment was made, I knew that I had only one more week of migraine headaches. One more week, that meant, five more days, then four more days, three, two and finally my last day. I felt good that last day. Nothing the prince or his entourage would do bothered me.

I did not inform the nursing agency that I was going to quit. I did not want anyone or anything to keep me from quitting. Now, here it was seven p.m. and I was giving my report for the last time. I gave the oncoming nurse the report while she cried. I left.

David was waiting for me at the front of the hospital. He was surprised when I walked to the car, opened the door and sat in front next to him. He asked me if I was ok. I told him to get going quick and I would tell him on the way home. On the way home, he asked me again if I was okay. I smiled at him and I told him I was fine. "No headache?" he asked. "No headache," I said. "No headaches, ever again. I quit," I told him as he sat there looking at me, not knowing what to think or say. He asked me if I was sure that is what I wanted to do. He reminded me that it was a good paying job. I told him I would wash dishes before I would go back to work taking care of that man and taking all the abuse from him and his entourage.

I got on the phone and called the nursing agency. I told them that I would not go back to work on Monday to take care of that man. They tried to talk me into going back, even offered me more money. I said no. They said they understood. And they did because I was the nurse that had stayed with the patient the longest.

I got my last paycheck from the nursing agency and gave it to David. He sent in the last payment on my last bill. It felt great. I do not know what felt better, the fact that I had paid off my last bill or the fact that I would not have to go back to that awful patient and his entourage. But I felt great. No more migraine headaches.

I took a week off and then I called the nursing agency to let them know I was ready to accept another case. They still could not find nurses that were willing to take care of the prince. All the nurses that were sent to care for him would last only one or two days. More money was offered by the nursing agency, but I could not do it. I did not ever want to work in a situation where I was treated as badly as I had been treated by the prince and his entourage. The way I was told that I could not finish my meal because the prince was ready "now", the way I had to wait outside the store because they did not want me to go in with them, the way I would have to crawl under the dining table to apply the TENS unit for his therapy because he specifically wanted the treatment done while he ate his noon meal, but the worst of all was the way they would look at me and "batha" (which is what it sounded like) me. By the look on their faces when they said that, I knew that it was not very nice. And now, it was over. No amount of money would get me to go back and work for them.

After a week of not working, I was ready to resume my work-life without the worry of the bills, knowing that whatever money I made, I could save now. But another week went by and I wondered if I would have to go work at a hospital. I did not want to be without work. There were still my child support payments, my rent and groceries.

Finally at the beginning of the second week of not working, I received a call from the nursing agency. They wanted to know if I would accept a case that might be at least for two weeks, doing private duty. I accepted. I did not want to go another week without work.

CHAPTER 23

1982 TO 1992

The patient for my next case was in the hospital but would be discharged within the next two days. I was going to do private duty nursing care taking care of a man in his home who had multiple sclerosis. Finally the day arrived on which I was instructed to go to the patient's home at three p.m. to start the evening shift.

I rang the door bell and was met at the door by the patient's responsible caregiver. I introduced myself and she let me into the house and to the living room. There was a middle age man, whom I found out later was forty-three years old, sitting in a recliner watching television. I walked up near the recliner and the caregiver introduced me to the patient. He took one look at me and told the caregiver that I needed to get out. He wanted a young, blond, blue-eyed nurse to care for him. Well here was a middle aged Hispanic man, mustache and slightly overweight. The caregiver explained to him that she would call the nursing agency next day, but for now, I would have to stay.

The patient would not look at me or talk to me. Once we put him to bed, all I had to do was give him his medications and turn him every two hours. He kept his eyes closed and I talked to him only when I had to. Usually, he would answer very angrily or just nod his head. I did my job by taking care of him and waited for eleven o'clock p.m. for the change of shift. The eleven o'clock nurse came in for the night shift. She was a younger nurse and the patient was pleased.

The next day, I was informed by the nursing agency that I needed to work the night shift because the nurse had quit due to the fact that it was too hard to turn the patient without help. The agency called me early in the morning asking me to please work the night shift as the patient felt that he could tolerate me better at night. He felt he would be asleep and he did not have to look at me. I showed up at eleven p.m. and worked the night shift. I worked the night shift for about two weeks.

The young nurses that were being sent by the nursing agency would work only one or two days and quit. You see, it took two persons to lift him out of bed to the wheelchair and from the wheelchair to the recliner. Because of his disease, every time that the patient was moved, he would have muscle spasms that would cause him to tighten his body up, making it extremely difficult to maintain a good hold on him while lifting him. His knees would contract and it was very difficult to get him to relax his body. The muscle spasms were so strong that if he caught the nurse's hand between his knees during the spasm, it could cause the nurse's hand to become bruised.

After two weeks, the agency was having a difficult time finding nurses to send to care for the patient. Now I was on the day shift working double shifts. By now the patient had accepted me to take care of him, and if the agency happened to send a nurse, he would request that I stay on the day shift. That was good for me, because I hated to work the night shift.

The patient had an interesting history. He had at one time played in the band for Elvis Presley. He would tell me interesting stories about the time he worked for Elvis. His favorite experience was when Elvis performed at what was the Rice Hotel in Houston. After the performance, girls were screaming and fighting to get to Elvis. The crowd of girls was pushing so hard that the security guards could not contain the crowd. Security decided that it was too risky to try to get Elvis to the limousine parked in front of the hotel, so security placed a hat on my patient, got some body guards to escort my patient out to the limousine parked in front while Elvis was taken out the back of the hotel. My patient said it was very exciting for him to see the crowd of girls trying to get to him. No one had noticed that it was him and not Elvis being escorted to the limousine.

In taking care of the patient doing double shifts, I got to work long hours and many days without a day off. On one occasion, I worked twelve hours a day for three months without a day off, and on several occasions, I worked thirty days without a day off. I enjoyed working and enjoyed making the amount of money I was making working all those days and hours.

As I said before, David took care of my finances. All I did was endorse my paycheck so he could deposit the check in the bank and I signed checks so he could write the checks and pay whatever needed to be paid.

Since I had paid all my bills and had been able to save a little bit of money, David told me that now I would have to work at getting my credit built back up. Due to all the bills I had been behind on, my credit was bad. So David instructed me to fill out an application for a Visa/Master credit card and to make a copy of the application. I sent the application for the credit card and kept the copy. We both knew I would be denied a credit card the first few times. Sure enough I was denied. David told me to wait a month and then send another application. The copy would be used to make sure that I had exactly the same information as the one before. And again I was denied.

Finally, on the third application, I received a Visa/MasterCard with a credit limit of four hundred dollars. David told me to use the card, but pay it off every month so that I would not pay interest. I applied for a JC Penny credit card and I was denied. I applied to American Express and I received a card. David told me to use the American Express card also but he was not too pleased that I had to pay annually for the card. But the card would help me get my credit to a good standing. And that is exactly what I did. Eventually, I discontinued the American Express card, but by now my credit was very good.

The private duty case that was supposed to have been for only two weeks had turned into several years. The patient was young and had been healthy and athletic prior to developing multiple sclerosis, so he was in good health except for the disease. By now he had gotten to where he required a feeding tube and continuous use of oxygen. That kept us from getting him out of bed, that and the fact that there was no one else in the house to help me get him out of bed. He was completely bed bound. He also had a tracheotomy performed and had the tracheostomy tube in place, connected to the oxygen.

The patient's brother lived out of town. The patient was completely dependent on the responsible party, who was the same lady that had been with him for many years. She handled all his financial business. She was good to him and made sure we took good care of him. As many years as he had been completely bed bound, his skin was completely intact. No red areas or broken skin areas. No bedsores. We were taking good care of him.

While I worked doing the private duty case, David asked me why I didn't go back to school and get my R.N. license. I had a lot of experience and was a very good nurse. Because I had tried twice before and not been able to complete my training due to financial problems, I told him I did not want to start school again and have to drop out as I had to do before. David told me that I could go to school if I wanted to complete my studies because the situation was different now. I did not have any bills to pay, only child support, rent, groceries and utilities and I would have time to study where I worked. After turning him every two hours, the patient would go to sleep. He had gotten to where he listened to music, which he enjoyed. He did not want me to read to him or do too much talking. In-between turning the patient, I had plenty of time to read and study. David felt I could make it.

CHAPTER 24

LOSS OF MY MOTHER

During this time of living in Houston and working long hours, I would try as often as I could to spend time with my parents. Twice a year, I would bring them to Houston for two weeks so that I could spend time with them and they spend time with me. My Father was not too excited about coming to Houston, but my Mother loved it. On one of the visits to Houston, my Father became ill and was in the hospital in the intensive care unit and I think that is why he did not look forward to coming to Houston.

My parents had never been to Houston and my Father was uneasy with the traffic. When I would take them out in the car, my Father would sit in the front seat with me. He would place his two hands on the dashboard and lean forward constantly commenting on the speed of the cars driving by and the heavy traffic.

After they had visited in Houston a few times, I decided that it was time for me to tell them that I was gay. I do not know whether they knew I was gay or whether they suspected I was gay or whether they had no idea. But I felt it was time for me to let them know about me.

The day I had decided to talk to them about me, I went to work in the morning as usual and came home at three in the afternoon. I entered my apartment and my Mother was sitting on one end of the sofa, knitting. My Mother loved sewing and crocheting. She could sit for hours, her glasses at the end of her nose, and her legs crossed at her ankles.

My Father was sitting at the other end of the sofa, dozing and watching television when he could stay awake. But most of the time, he dozed. If you asked him if he slept during the day, he would always say that he never slept during the day.

I greeted them as I walked across the room into the bedroom to change clothes. After I had changed clothes I came into the room where they were still sitting, with my Father awake and asking about my work.

After some light talk and my Mother still knitting, I told them I wanted to talk to them. I pulled up a chair to sit in front of them. My Mother stopped her knitting and placed her hands on her lap.

I had put a lot of thought into deciding if I should tell my parents about my being gay. I knew it would hurt them and I hated the thought of them hurting. I kept wondering how I should tell them, how to tell them, and what words to use in Spanish to tell them. I am not too polished at using certain Spanish words and was certain I knew the correct words to use.

In Spanish I told them that the reason I had gotten a divorce was because I was homosexual. I did not know the Spanish word for gay. That is all I said. For a few seconds there was silence. I guess they were expecting me to say more, but that is all I could think of to say.

My Mother then repeated "and that is why you got a divorce? Margie is a wonderful woman and we did not understand why you had gotten a divorce. Now we know." Then she looked at me, with her glasses still at the end of her nose and said, "You are my son and I love you no matter what." Then she continued her knitting.

My Father sat there as if in deep thought, scratching his bald head and said, "Does this mean we don't go to the zoo?" I had told them we would go to the zoo this evening and that was why I had come home from work early. We went to the zoo.

Nothing was ever said about my being gay after that. My Mother went on as usual and did house work, cooked, and would wash all my clothes while they were here visiting.

My Mother was a great cook and enjoyed cooking for her family. She also enjoyed teaching and would teach anyone that wanted to learn to cook.

Some friends of mine knew that my Mother knew how to make tamales and they also knew she would be coming to visit soon. They asked me if Mamasita, as they called her, would teach them how to make tamales. I asked my Mother and she was very happy they had asked.

My friends, six of them and all of them gay, provided everything that was needed for the tamales. My Mother had told them that they had to start early to be through by at least two in the afternoon. They were at my apartment by seven in the morning. My Mother had already cooked the meat the evening before and soaked the corn husks.

My Mother had a great fun time trying to teach my friends. They all helped in setting up to make the tamales and all stood around the table taking turns making the tamales. They each had on an apron and being gay, you can imagine what some of the aprons looked like. Most of the aprons had flowers and ruffles.

My Father and I stayed away and just watched. With all the talking going on and my Mother frequently laughing so hard she would have to move away from the table, my Father would say, "they are all crazy and so is your Mother."

Finally by about two in the afternoon the first pot of tamales was cooked and we all ate. The tamales were good. My friends talked about what they had just gotten through learning. They all helped clean the kitchen and they each got to take several dozen tamales home. My Mother never forgot about my friends and each time they came to visit, my friends would come by and visit with Mamasita.

As I had said before, David felt that I should go back to school and felt I could make it. But before I could decide to go back to school, my dear, sweet Mother became ill.

My Mother had been a diabetic for a long time and a year prior to this illness, one of her kidneys had stopped functioning. She was admitted to the hospital in Brady. My Mother had no insurance so I had to pay the hospital bill. The doctor informed me that the kidney would have to be removed, so I transferred her to Galveston to the hospital. The hospital bill in Brady had been almost sixteen thousand dollars for the two weeks she was there. In Galveston, after the surgery to remove the kidney and a two week stay, it only cost me four dollars.

During my Mother's hospital stay in Galveston, I went to work on the night shift still taking care of the same patient. Every morning my Father and I would drive to Galveston to be with my Mother and stay until evening, then come home so I could go work. My Father wanted to visit with my Mother during the day and I would sleep on the recliner.

After my Mother was discharged from the hospital, the doctor said that he wanted me to wait to take my Mother back to Brady until after he saw her again in three weeks. So I brought my parents to the garage apartment and I would sleep in David's apartment. David was very helpful with my parents. He would cook for them and make sure they were eating well. I had returned to working the day shift after my Mother was discharged from the hospital.

My Mother did well and soon David and I drove them back to Brady. The bad news was that the doctor had told us that my Mother's other kidney was not functioning well and that sooner or later it would stop functioning. If that happened, my Mother would have to be on dialysis.

My Mother had had at one time two friends who had been on dialysis before they died and my Mother had helped care for them. My Mother had told us that she did not want to be on dialysis and if it meant that she would die, then so be it. All this was in the early part of 1986. All she was praying for was to be able for her and my Father to celebrate their 50th wedding anniversary.

Their anniversary was celebrated in August 1987. I made sure that a big celebration of their 50th anniversary was held in Brady. My Father and my Mother repeated their vows in a mass ceremony at the Melvin Catholic Church. After the mass, we celebrated in Brady with the friends that my Mother had invited. We also held a dance for her and I got to dance with her and I got to see her and my Father dance. I had never seen them dance. My Mother went home early because she was tired, but she had a very good time. Some of her sisters even came from North Texas to be with her.

My daughter, Nelda, graduated from high school and had come to Houston to live with me. After a short while, she went back to Abilene. Shortly after that, I was informed that Nelda had moved in with some man she had been dating. My daughter living with a man and not being married was not exactly what I had wanted for her, but she was of age and she had to make her own decisions.

After living with the man for a while I was informed that I would be a grandfather. I was very happy. I always wanted to be a grandfather. When I saw Nelda, I told her that the only thing I was asking from them is that I did not want my grandchild to be born out of wedlock. So Nelda and the man got married. They got married here in Houston in the house I was living in. She was already seven months pregnant and only a few people, lesbian and gay friends of mine, and my parents were in attendance. The friends had been invited by me and they were happy for me. Nelda received only baby presents on her wedding day.

My granddaughter, Ashley, was born March 29, 1988, in New Braunfels, Texas. I drove to Brady and took my Mother and Father with me to see my granddaughter. My Mother had already been having problems with her heart and had been prescribed heart medication. My Mother was very happy to see my granddaughter. She held the baby and I took a picture. I took my parents back to Brady and I came home to Houston. I instructed my older sister to watch my Mother closely and to take her to the doctor if she became ill.

I came back to Houston and went back to work. I had worked for one week when my older sister called me and told me that my Mother was in the hospital. I told David and he told me to go see my Mother. I drove to Brady to the hospital and saw my Mother and visited with her. She was being treated for congestive heart failure. I visited with her all afternoon until visiting hours were over. I went with my Father and older sister.

At about two o'clock in the morning, a nurse called from the hospital and stated that my Mother had taken a turn for the worse and had been transferred to the intensive care unit of the hospital. My Father, older sister and I got dressed and went back to the hospital. My Mother was awake but was confused. She would talk but not make sense of what she was saying.

My Father, older sister and I had decided that I would stay at night at the hospital while they went home to rest. During the day I could go home and rest while my Father and sister would stay at the hospital. My Mother's older brother and his wife came in from out of town to see my Mother. I ended staying all day and all night with my Mother so that my sister could help with my uncle and his wife. I would go home to shower and change, and then go back to the hospital. I would catch a few minutes of sleep here and there whenever I could.

During one of the nights that I was staying with my Mother at the hospital, I was sitting at her bed side reading the Bible while she slept. All was quiet and I began to get sleepy. I decided to get up and walk so that I would not fall asleep.

During my walk down the hall I realized I was very tired. I got to the door to enter the Intensive Care Unit where my Mother was and I stood at the door and prayed. I prayed to God that it was His will regarding my Mother's health but to give me strength to help my Father and my sisters. From that moment on, I felt the strength to do what needed to be done and did not feel tired or weary.

The doctor then told us that he wanted to transfer my Mother to San Angelo hospital where they would be more able to meet her needs. The Brady hospital was a small hospital and did not have the proper equipment necessary to care for extremely sick patients like my Mother. An ambulance transferred my Mother to San Angelo. My three sisters, my Father, my uncle and aunt went to the hospital in San Angelo with me.

My Mother got worse and on Friday morning my dear sweet Mother died. April 15, 1988. I went through the whole process of making funeral arrangements, seeing and talking to people that came to pay their respects. My Mother was a very loving, caring lady and had many friends.

The day of her funeral was a very cold day. Her body was taken to the church in Melvin and she was buried in the Melvin cemetery. There were a lot of people at the funeral. I was very surprised at the number of people that attended her funeral even on a cold day.

A few days after the funeral I came back to Houston and continued to work. Now I had to work as much as I could again. I had paid for my Mother's funeral and I was paying my Mother's hospital bill in Brady from the time she had been transferred to Galveston and had a kidney removed. I wanted to pay my Mother's bills because I knew my Father could not afford to pay and I did not want anyone bothering my Father for payments he could not make. I had been able to save some money and was able to pay for my Mother's funeral. I also bought a beautiful headstone with her name and a place for my Father's name when he too died.

As I drove back home to Houston, I noticed that I did not feel tired. I thought about my prayer in the hospital and realized that after my prayer, I was able to go through my Mother's death, funeral arrangements, meeting and greeting people and through the funeral without feeling tired. My faith in God grew much stronger.

CHAPTER 25

GOING BACK TO SCHOOL

I continued working with the same case that I had been on for several years now. I worked the twelve hour shifts and on many occasions worked several weeks and up to thirty days without a day off. I did not mind and I needed the money.

I had paid the hospital bill in Brady and I was now able to save most of my money. David started pushing for me to go to school to obtain my license as a registered nurse. I felt I may be too old since I was forty-two years old now. David told me I was not too old and to go to school.

And so I started taking classes and continued working. Getting back to taking classes was not as hard as I thought it would be. Because I had plenty of time to read and study helped to make it easier for me. But then came the time for me to start doing my nursing tour of duty at the hospitals during the day. The responsible person for my patient did some brainstorming and I was able to keep my job and go to school at the same time. I would work sixteen hours on Saturdays and Sundays, from seven in the morning to eleven at night. During the week, I would work some evenings depending on the class schedule.

I had started taking care of the patient in 1982 and continued to take care of him until 1991. In 1991, the patient's brother decided to have the patient transferred to where the brother lived so that they could see each other more often. The patient asked me if I would move to the same city so that I could continue to care for him. I thanked him but told him that I liked Houston and could not move and live anywhere else. And so he was transferred.

By now I was getting ready to graduate from nursing school. It had been three years of taking classes and working the long weekends, but now at last, I was going to graduate. It had not been easy. I was forty-five years old and I was finally realizing my dream. I was going to be able to take the boards and receive my license as a registered nurse. I had to pass the state boards first, but I was determined that I was going to pass the boards. I had come too far and gone through too much hardship to fail now.

Getting through the college courses had not been easy. I even took a G.E.D. math/algebra class to help me through the college math classes. Taking the G.E.D. class helped me but also set me behind a semester. It was frustrating and disappointing for me, but David was there to encourage me and make sure I did not give up.

My dear, sweet David was so wonderful to me while I was going to school. He would help me to study, but it made me feel discouraged at times. You see, David knew all the answers to my test questions and homework. He did not read or even look at my books and he knew the answers. He would see how I would struggle to get the correct answer to a question and he would give me the answer, but he always tried to make it look like I had gotten the answer by myself. My dear precious friend, I loved him.

On graduation day, David kept telling me how proud he was of me and that I had accomplished this all by myself. I knew I had not. If it had not been for him, I would not have gotten this far. In fact, without him, I would not have even started. But David helped me to gain the courage I needed to go to school. Working the hours I worked while going to school, David made it easier for me by fixing supper for us, doing laundry, grocery shopping and of course, taking care of my finances. I was able to make the rent payments but he always told me not to worry about the rent if I was not able to work. Since most nurses had not been able to take care of the patient because he was hard to take care of physically, I had more than enough work.

Now that I had graduated, I had to study for the State Board nursing exam. I studied every minute I had free time because to me, this was it. No time to fail. David would make sure I was studying and every time he came to my apartment and did not find me sitting with a book in front of me, he would ask me why I was not studying.

Now it was time for me to go to Austin and take my State Board exams. I was excited and nervous, but David kept reassuring me that I would do well. He reminded me to "go pee" before the exams. He and I had discussed hearing somewhere that a person could do better on a test if that person emptied their bladder prior to taking the test. I assured him I would and I went on to take my Boards.

Taking the State Board exams was not as difficult as I thought it would be. I felt confident that I had done well the first day of exams. The other students I had gone to Austin with all felt that it was hard and that they were not sure they had done well. Some even said that they had failed for sure. I began to feel uneasy because as hard a time as I had in school, I felt I knew the right answers to the questions and I did not feel the exam was that difficult.

After the second day of exams, we all piled into the two cars we had driven to Austin in and drove back to Houston, going over and over the questions and answers. By the time we got to Houston, most of the students felt they had failed the exams. By now, I was not too sure I had done well. We were all supposed to be adults, especially me, since I was the oldest one among the students in my group. We were all behaving like young school kids. We all agreed to call each other after we heard the results from the Boards.

David came over and asked about the State Board exams and if I felt I had done well. I told him that maybe I had, but I was not sure at all. I told him that if I received a large brown envelope from the State Board of Nursing Exams that it meant I failed. Somewhere I had heard, or maybe we were told at the exams, that if we failed the exams, we would be notified and provided with registration forms in a large brown envelope to apply for a second exam. I told him that if I received a large brown envelope, I did not even want to see it. I was being childish at age forty plus, but I think it was more out of frustration. What if I failed?

I went to work in a hospital while I waited for the State Board results. As graduate students, we were provided with a temporary license to practice as graduate nurses. If

I passed, I would immediately become and be known as a registered nurse.

Every day, except Sundays, David would go downstairs to get the mail from the mailbox and look through the mail to see if I had received any notice from the State Board. Every time he came in, he would call from the bottom of the stairs, "Nothing from the State Board". If I was in my apartment, he would call me and let me know that I had not received notice yet.

It was on a Saturday mid-afternoon when I was in my apartment and the phone rang. David wanted me to come over for a minute. It never occurred to me that it might be something concerning the State Board results. I came in the back door and David was sitting in his brown leather recliner that was placed almost in the middle of the room facing the television. He always sat there to eat, watch television or take care of finances and bills.

I walked in and sat down on the sofa on the side nearest the recliner. This was a very frequent routine for us. Still not thinking it may be about the exams, I looked at him and asked why he had called me. He looked at me and said, "Now Joe, no matter what happens, if you failed the exams, you will take them again. You hear me?" I stood up and said, "I failed, I failed. Is it a large brown envelope?" He looked at me with a sad expression on his face as he nodded yes. He handed me the envelope and I did not take it. I was devastated. I could not open the envelope. I started to walk to the door. David asked me to at least open it and make sure. I told him I did not care anymore and did not want the envelope. As I walked out the back door, he asked if I wanted him to open the envelope. I answered "I don't care what you do with it. I don't want to see it."

I went inside my apartment and sat down thinking, what am I going to do now? I don't know if I could go through this again. I sat there feeling numb. Gosh, I failed.

I heard footsteps coming down the walkway from David's apartment to my door. I could always hear his footsteps on the wooden walkway because he seemed to always walk with a thump sound to each step. He knocked on the door and when I did not answer, he came in. He always did that, knocked on the door and if I did not answer or go open the door for him, he always came in anyway. It did not bother me.

"Joe, take a look at this. It looks like a license, with your name on it stating you are a registered nurse." David said in a voice that sounded hesitant and unsure. I looked at it and it was my license as a registered nurse. I read the letter that was sent with the license, congratulating me on passing the boards. I looked at David and he looked at me. "I passed." I said going towards David and hugging him. Then we both cried. I kept repeating "thank you, thank you." as David congratulated me. Wow, I was an R.N. After all this years, I was a registered nurse. Wow!

I felt pure happiness. David was very happy for me and he took me out to eat. Wherever I wanted to go eat he said. It was his treat. Celebrating, he called it. I chose Luby's Cafeteria. We both enjoyed eating there. It was good enough for me.

Now I could work in areas of nursing that I was not able to work before because it required an R.N. license for the job. Now I could apply for a job that I had always felt I could do and could do better than some of the nurses in those positions.

I had always enjoyed working with geriatrics. That was always my favorite area in nursing and I had hoped I could someday work in that area. I continued working in the hospital but kept looking at the want ads for positions as a director of nurses in a nursing home. I felt I could be in management, and that I knew how to do the work. I could learn whatever I did not know. It seemed that nursing homes always needed director of nurses for their facilities.

I decided to apply at a small nursing home in a suburb of Houston. I chose that nursing home because it was small, even though I had to drive about thirty miles one way. I knew I had very little chance of getting the job because the ad called for experience in nursing home and I did not have that. But I would have to give it a try.

I drove the thirty miles to the nursing home and was there at least thirty minutes before my appointment time. I walked around the facility looking at the place. It was an old building, but small and the employees seemed nice. Every employee seemed to be very busy and I thought to myself that I don't mind the hard, fast paced work. I liked what I saw.

I sat in front of the desk waiting for the administrator to get through reading my resume. She finally put the resume down and started with the questions that I had prepared myself for. Finally the statement that I knew would be made, "You have not been a registered nurse for very long and you have no experience working in a nursing home and especially as a director of nurses." She asked me why she should hire me. I did my best to answer honestly and directly. "I enjoy working with geriatric people. I am hard working, very dependable. Even though I have only been a registered nurse for a short while, I have very good and valuable experience. I do not mind getting my hands dirty and what I do not know as a director of nurses, I am a very fast learner. I feel I am and have always been a damned good nurse and I feel that if someone does not hire me, it will be their loss. If you give me a chance, I can prove to you that what I have said is all true." I finished and sat there looking at her. I thought she was going to be upset, especially about it being her loss if she did not hire. I thought I had over done it.

The administrator finally said she had other interviews and would let me know. I asked when I would hear from her. This was a Tuesday afternoon. She said she would let me know by next Monday. That would be in six days I thought as I thanked her and walked to the car. Well, I thought, at least I gave it a try.

David asked me about the interview but I told him I did not feel I would get the job because of my lack of experience. We both agreed that eventually I would get a job at a nursing home. I would keep working at the hospital and wait until I had a few years of experience as a registered nurse, then I could try again.

Thursday evening of that same week I had a message on my telephone voice machine. Cell phones were not popular at the time. It was from the nursing home. The administrator wanted to know if I could come in for another interview. The next day, I called and set up for the second interview. I got the job.

I had a lot to learn as the director of nurses at the nursing home. It was hard work, much harder than working at the hospital. I enjoyed learning and did not mind the hard work. In order to be able to complete my work on a daily basis, I would help the nurses and nurses aides with the patient care in the morning until one in the afternoon. The afternoon was my time to complete my work. I was off weekends but called everyday to check with the charge nurse and make sure everything was going well.

I have had several years of experience in nursing homes since that first time. I have enjoyed working in the nursing homes because I felt I made a difference. I treated my nursing staff with respect and tried to help as much as I could. The nurse aides' work is very hard in a nursing home. And they are one of the most disrespected and lowest paid employees. Nursing homes get a bad reputation because the owners become greedy and make employee cuts to the point that hurts the patient and the facility.

At the last nursing home I worked, I refused to send nursing staff home because our census was low. If I sent my nurse aides home, they would go and look for work at a place that could use them all the time. It was extremely hard to get good, dependable workers. I felt that the employees that worked in the office should take their turn in going home to keep cost down. And so it was done.

Around this time my son, David, had graduated from high school and he came to live with me and go to school. He and I would ride together to attend classes at San Jacinto College. I was proud of my son going to school and also working part time.

One thing that I remember when we used to ride together is when we had a flat tire on our way to class. I pulled into the parking lot of a grocery store to change the tire. My son and I opened the trunk of the car and started getting the spare tire and tools out of the trunk. My son told me to place the jack under the car and jack the car up. I placed the jack in the place where I knew it was supposed to be placed. I started working at raising the car up, but the car was not going up. I kept turning the crank on the jack, but the only thing that was happening was the jack was going down into the ground. I told my son that I did not know what was wrong. He came over to check and see what the problem was.

He took a look at the jack as I had placed it under the car. The only thing he said was "Oh" as he cranked the jack down and pulled it out from under the car. I asked what was wrong as I saw him pull the jack from under the car and turn the jack right side up. I had placed the jack upside down and when I cranked the jack, it would just go into the ground. I felt so much love for my son because he did not make an issue or laugh. He just proceeded to change the tire. We got to class on time.

Also, my son had met and was dating the girl that later became his wife. My son had come and asked me if I could go eat with him and a girl he met. I realized then that this may be serious, since he had never introduced me to any girl he dated. We went to eat and I got to meet Jackie. They dated for a while and then David told me he had joined the Marines. By this time David and Jackie had decided to live together and they were renting an apartment in west Houston. My son went to the Marines and was in California. When he came back, Jackie and I went to meet him at the airport. He was skinny.

I did not like the idea of my son being in the service, but he was of age and I had to go along with what he wanted to do. When he completed his training, he came back to Houston and was in the reserves. He and Jackie decided to get married. David and Jackie's wedding was a very nice event. They got married in the Catholic Church, had a big reception and a big dance. It was all very nice. They went on a short honeymoon and soon they were on a routine schedule of married life.

Nelda came to live in Houston when Michael was nine months old. Michael's father had been in the Navy and Michael was born in Philadelphia. Michael was really cute and I enjoyed carrying him. David liked pushing Michael in the stroller and enjoyed seeing him be mischievous. Now I had both my son and daughter and their families living in Houston near me where I could enjoy seeing them and enjoy spending time with my grandchildren.

On December 30, 1992, David and Jackie had their first baby. My granddaughter Meghan was born. I was in the waiting room with several other people who were there waiting for their babies to be born. Finally, Meghan was born. She had a head full of dark, black hair just like her father had when he was born. It felt good being a grandfather. I was very happy and proud being a grandfather.

CHAPTER 26

1993 – 1998

After working in the nursing homes, I worked for a home health agency and learned how to manage the agency. I also enjoyed working in home health because we took care of mostly elderly people. I got to meet some wonderful senior people and spend time with those that were lonely and just needed someone to visit with them.

Here is how I learned home health and to manage a home health agency. In 1993, I was offered a job by a total stranger that was starting his own home health agency. The man was extremely nice and very ambitious. He was doing very well without the home health business, and I wondered why he would want to start a home health agency. But whatever the reason, I am glad he did because I learned so much from my experiences through working for him and from where I went from there.

During this time, home health was becoming a booming business and it was a lot easier starting a home health business. Medicare made it very easy for home health agencies to be started by almost anyone and that is what has happened in the home health business. There are a lot of very crooked people that love to steal from the government, and anyone, for that matter. The government has made tremendous changes since 1993, but probably billions of dollars too late.

The man who hired me to work for his agency had hired this old woman who was as evil as evil can be. But she wore a disguise. Her disguise was that of a sweet, elderly woman with gray hair and a sweet, soft voice, sugar and spice and everything nice except for the evil underneath.

After alerting the new boss as to what this woman was, he got rid of her but not until after we went to court as she claimed that she owned the agency. She lost in court. After that, she got someone else to start a home health agency where she ended going to prison for fraud. Hopefully when she gets out of prison, she will be too old to do any more harm to people.

In 1995, David encouraged me to open my own home health agency. Along with me as an owner, I made the big mistake of bringing in the male equivalent of the old evil lady. He was worthless, a con artist, and we kept the agency for a short time. Medicare made some big changes and we would have to make big changes in our company also. I was tired of having to baby sit my business partner so I chose to sell the business. And so we did. I never was sorry about selling the business. Some things are not worth having if it brings you nothing but grieve and anger.

Some very good things happened during the time I owned the home health agency. I got to work with some of the most wonderful caring nurses. The nurses and office employees were always willing to do work beyond what was required by their job. They were always willing to care for patients with AIDS during the time that people were so frightened about AIDS and even some nurses were afraid. The one thing I regretted in selling the agency was that I would not get to work with these wonderful people anymore. I will always remember them and think about them often.

After selling the agency, David and I agreed that I should take at least a couple of months off to rest. I never took vacations during all these years that I worked. When I would accumulate vacation time at my place of employment, I would take the vacation pay and not take any time off. I did not care to travel and I never had any special places to go, so I never took a vacation. I was fine with that. I preferred to work.

After becoming a registered nurse, I felt I had accomplished a goal I had set for myself through the help of my dear friend. But I always kept in mind a person in my past that was very important in encouraging me to be successful. Because of this person, I kept telling myself that I had to continue on with getting my education. Just as my thinking that I wanted to graduate from high school and finishing business school to go work in a bank got me through high school, this person has helped get me to where I am now.

That person was my high school English teacher who had given me her school picture where she wrote on the back of the picture, *To Joe, who will succeed in life.* Throughout the years of my struggles to get the education I wanted, I would think of those words that my English teacher had written on the back of her picture. It was not only what she wrote, she had also shown that she cared. It was in many little things that she said or did that she showed she cared. I will always remember that she told me she liked reading my essays because what I wrote had depth and it made her have to think.

In October 1995, I drove to the town where I had last heard she was living. Or at least to the town where I had last heard she had taught. I had no idea how I would find her but I felt that I might find someone who might have known her.

Once I got to Waxahachie, the last town I had heard she had taught school, I started to think about how I could find my former school teacher. I decided that maybe if I went to the high school and ask at the office, someone might still know something about her. When I got to the school office, I walked in and a lady told me that she would be with me in a minute. Once she got through with what she was doing, she asked in what way she could help me. I gave her my name and explained to her that I was looking for a lady who had taught me when I was in high school and that I had heard she had taught at this school. I asked if she knew where I could find her. She said the teacher I was looking for was still teaching there and that she was teaching a class as we spoke. She told me she would send a note to her, if I could wait there in the office.

As I sat down to wait for the teacher, I became nervous. I wondered if she remembered me. I felt she probably would not remember since she had probably taught thousands of students since I was in school. It had been thirty years.

I did not have to wait too long. My English teacher walked in. She looked exactly as she did thirty years ago, except for the gray hair. She still wore short hair and had a strong handshake. Still the same as how she looked years ago. She told me she had to finish the class and then she could leave. She walked me to the study hall where I saw her husband. He, too, looked the same, again except for the gray hair. This was wonderful. I had no trouble finding these wonderful, beautiful people.

My English teacher's husband and I sat in the study hall and visited while we waited for her to finish her class. I told him why I wanted to find his wife and how those words on that picture had encouraged me to continue my education. I told him a small part of my struggles to get my education and how I felt I have been successful. He told me I should talk to young children and teenagers. He felt that my story could be an inspiration to young children.

The three of us went to eat at a Mexican restaurant and we visited while we ate. At the restaurant she ordered "lengua" and highly recommended "lengua" (lengua is tongue). After we ate, they invited me to their home. It was on a Wednesday evening and I had forgotten that they may be going to church, as he was a preacher. My English teacher's husband went on to church and she and I stayed and we visited. It was about ten o'clock when I left and I felt badly that I had kept her from going to church. But I was also very happy to have had the visit with her. I thanked her for the words on the back of the picture.

The next morning before I left to come back home to Houston, I stopped at a flower shop and sent her a beautiful corsage. The lady at the flower shop knew my former English teacher and I told her why I had come to see her. I went home very happy thanking God for allowing me to be able to thank this lady and with no trouble at finding her.

My Lord had made it all so easy. I guess because He knew how much I needed to do this.

A few days later I received a letter from my English teacher. She thanked me for the flowers and for the visit. She stated that she had enjoyed the story about the tambourine.

In the letter was a picture of her and one of her husband. Since then, that letter and their pictures are framed and they hang in my home where others can see their pictures and I can tell them how her words inspired me to reach my goals.

The story about the tambourine was as follows. A pastor friend of mine from a gospel church here in Houston and I had met at a grocery store. While we were visiting he invited me to come back to his church, as I had visited a few times. I told him I was always wishing I could play a tambourine, as I had always been amused by how the people there kept in time with the music with their tambourines. On the Sunday that I visited the church several weeks later, the music was playing, people were standing, singing and clapping their hands. When he saw me walk in and find my place on one of the rows of pews, he announced loudly, "Someone please give Brother Joe a tambourine. He wants to make joyful noises unto the Lord." He had remembered. Someone did give me a large tambourine and I just held on to it, not knowing how to use it.

The singing went on for a while and I just held on to the tambourine afraid to make noise. Then it was time for the sermon. The pastor started preaching the sermon. I had placed the tambourine on my lap and halfway through the sermon when everyone was quiet and the pastor was preaching his sermon, I dropped the tambourine on the wooden floor. It made the loudest noise. The pastor stopped the sermon and said loudly through the microphone, "Thank God, Brother Joe has made joyful noises unto the Lord." Everyone stood up and started clapping and singing, the instruments started playing and I sat there very embarrassed by having dropped the tambourine.

On December 5, 1996, my son's second daughter, Madison, was born. My dear, sweet Madison. This baby could cry, and cry she did. But I still baby sat and eventually she grew old enough to where she would not cry when I took care of her.

CHAPTER 27

NOVEMBER 1998

As I had mentioned before, David and I had agreed that I would take a couple of months off of work so that I could rest. My rest period was of two weeks duration. I noticed in the want ads that a nursing home needed a registered nurse for their Minimum Data Sets (MDS) department. I felt I could do that job. I talked with David and told him I wanted that job. He told me if I felt I wanted to go back to work, do it. I applied for and got the job. The job required having to in-put patient information in the computer and complete patient information assessments. I was not good at working with computers but I felt I could do the job. I had never done any of that work before, but I felt I could learn it fast. And so I learned the job quickly and I did a good job. It was easy and I enjoyed doing the work.

On October 22, 1998, I got home after work and my daughter met me at the doorway to the apartment. She told me that David had an accident and was taken to the emergency room by ambulance. They did not have my work telephone number and could not get in touch with me. I asked for the name of the hospital and immediately drove to the hospital.

When I got to the hospital emergency room, I walked to the reception desk. I explained to the receptionist that my landlord had an accident and was brought here by ambulance. I gave her his name and she informed me that only his family could go back to see him. She told me I could wait in the waiting room. When I looked at the waiting room, the room was packed. I did not want to wait, I wanted to see David. I had to find a way to see David.

I turned to her and told her that David was my significant other. She immediately walked me to the room where David was laying on a gurney or stretcher as most people call them. A nurse was in there with David and she asked me how I was related to the patient. I told her that I was his significant other. She told me to wait there and immediately she came back with two doctors who wanted to talk to me. They asked me about his medications, his allergies and illnesses. They said they had wanted to do an MRI and other tests but that they needed permission to have that done and to know about his past history.

They took David to do the MRI and tests they wanted to do and I went to call David's sister that lived in the state of Oklahoma. When I talked to her, I explained what I had been told by a witness that was with David at the time of the accident. David had been trimming the branches of the pecan tree that was in the front yard of the house. David was overweight and when he climbed the ten foot ladder that was placed on the grass, the ladder began to sink into the ground. As the ladder was sinking into the ground, the ladder began to lean to the side until it fell to the side.

David fell and landed on the sidewalk, his head hitting on the sidewalk. He had tried to get up but started to fall again. The neighbor called 911 and the ambulance people transferred him to the emergency room. According to the neighbor, David also had seizures while they waited for the ambulance. David's sister told me she would be coming in as soon as she could get a flight and asked if I could pick her up at the airport. I told her I would.

After I talked with David's sister, I went up to the ICU where David would be transferred after the MRI. The nurses in the ICU were very nice and caring towards David. He was confused and his words that he tried to speak were not words but just gibberish. But he recognized me and would call me by my name. He would do things for me when I asked him to, for example, to turn, to look upward or to look to the sides.

The doctors had come to check on him and told me that there had been some bleeding in his head. They were monitoring the bleeding in case they had to do surgery to relieve the pressure. They were not sure as to the extent of damage there would be, if any. They would have to do other MRIs and tests to monitor the bleeding.

The nurses would allow me to go into the ICU area any time that I wanted to because I would be a big help to them with David. The nurses noticed that David would look at me and call out my name each time I came to his bedside. He would try to talk but I did not understand what he was saying. But he would follow my commands when I would ask him to do something for me and that, in itself, was a great positive sign related to his injury. I would shave him and assist the nurse with his bath and in changing the bed.

I stayed all night at the hospital and was there in the morning when the doctors made their rounds. They explained to me that they were going to continue more MRIs and test to continue monitoring the bleeding. So far, the bleeding did not seem to have increased from the last tests they had done.

During the night while I waited in the waiting room, I prayed for David. I prayed to God to please help David. I prayed to my Lord that His will be done as far as David's health, but to give me the strength to help David. After prayer, I felt relaxed. I knew that David would be okay.

David's sister arrived at the airport and I was there to pick her up and bring here to the hospital. When we got to the hospital, they allowed both of us to go in to see David. He did not seem to recognize his sister. We stayed there a while and then we went home agreeing to come early next morning so she could talk to the doctors.

On the way home, David's sister stated that he did not look like he would be well again. She felt he would be a vegetable the rest of his life. She felt that everything was much worse than she expected. She would make sure to talk to the doctors in the morning.

Early the next morning, we went to the hospital to see David. The doctors had not come in yet and the nurse had stated that there had been no change in David's condition. So we waited in the waiting room a few minutes. While sitting in the waiting room, she stated that after she spoke with the doctors, she would call her husband to come to

Houston and help her. She felt that David's house would have to be put up for sale and he would have to be moved to where she lived and probably he would need someone to take care of him the rest of his life.

We went back in to be with David. In a few minutes, the doctors came to make their rounds. When the doctors came in, they talked about David's condition. They explained to her the same thing they had explained to me, that they were monitoring to make sure there was not any more bleeding. If it showed on the tests that he had more bleeding, then they would have to do surgery to relieve any pressure to the brain. The tests would continue to be done as long as they felt necessary to monitor the bleeding. It was a waiting situation for now.

After the doctors left, we went to a conference room so David's sister could call her husband to ask him to come to Houston. They would put the house up for sale, her husband would drive David's car back to Oklahoma and she would transfer David by airplane to the hospital in the city where she lived.

I was devastated. I did not want to lose my dearest friend. He was going to be okay. I believed that God had heard my prayers. David recognized me every time I went to see him. He knew who I was. He had to be okay.

Late, that afternoon, the doctors made their rounds. David's sister explained to the doctors that she was going to transfer him to a hospital in Oklahoma. The doctor explained that right at this moment, they were monitoring for further bleeding and that it was too risky for David to be transferred. The doctor told her that when David got to a point where he could be transferred without risks, then he would approve the transfer.

From October 22 through the 29th I went to see David every day, twice a day. I would stop by on my way to work and then in the evening. David's sister had learned her way to the hospital, so she would drive herself to see David. She and I had agreed that she would visit David in the morning and I would visit in the evening.

When I went in the evenings to see him, I would notice that he could say more words than he had been able to say the previous day. The nurses encouraged me to talk to him because he would try harder at mouthing words. He could always say my name. He had no problem with that.

On October 30th, David seemed much more alert. For the first time after the accident he sat on the side of the bed. David dangled his feet on the side of the bed, assisting us in sitting him up and then laying him back down. David would respond to me more readily than he would respond to the nurses. He still had periods of restlessness and periods of talking at random, in other words, just talked. But there was great improvement. In a patient with brain trauma, any time the patient is able to follow one small command, or one correct response, or one small positive action or word response, it is a great improvement. It may not seem like much to the non-medical person, but it means a lot to the medical staff. David seemed to be showing great improvement.

David was improving every day. He still talked at random at times, but the doctor had said that all that might improve once the swelling in his brain went down. David and I could converse to a certain extent. I could ask him to sit on the side of the bed and he would follow command. He had difficulty with words, but I would encourage him to keep on trying until he would say the word or words.

David was in the ICU for sixteen days when the doctors felt that he should be transferred to the rehab center. Houston has one of the best rehab centers in the world. He was transferred out of ICU to one of the floors in the same hospital until they could get him a room at the rehab center. David could now feed himself and sit on the side of the bed by himself. He continued having difficulty with words, but still he had improved greatly.

Because of the brain trauma, David would use words that he never would have used in front of anyone, especially in front of his sister. He never was combative, but just used colorful words. That was something he never did before the accident, at least, not often.

David was transferred to the rehab center in the Houston's medical center. Once he transferred there, we were instructed that visitors were not welcomed during the day so that they could have uninterrupted time to work with David. Visiting hours were in the evening. I went every evening to see him. I could see that he was improving more every day. I would ask him to call out phone numbers that I knew he had memorized before the accident. I would have him tell me the names of the neighbors, people he had worked with, names of my family that he knew. He could remember most of the names and phone numbers.

David meant the world to me. My dearest friend, I loved him dearly and I was devastated by what he was going through. I knew that he had improved greatly from the time I saw him in the emergency room after the accident up to now. I kept talking to him about things in his life that he had talked to me about, his mother, his father, his little brother and his sister, whom he had always talked about with love and pride.

David had told me about times past in his life and now I was using that information to help him remember, so that he could think. I also talked to him about the present, about things we had done together and places we had gone to eat together. Because he could remember a lot of the past and much of the present, I knew that he would get well.

I am a Christian and I believe in the Lord. I had faith that the Lord would help David through this. Even though David did not go to church, I know he believed in God. He knew the Bible and often, he and I would listen to the sermons on television.

The Lord works in mysterious ways. It was a few days before Thanksgiving of 1998 and David's sister talked to the doctors at the rehab center about her going back home for the holiday and then coming back. They agreed, feeling that this was the perfect time for her to go home. Since visitors were restricted to certain hours and David was not ready to be discharged, they encouraged her to go home.

David's sister made the airplane reservation, packed her bags and I drove her to the airport. She said goodbye voicing that she would be back after the Thanksgiving holidays.

David continued to improve tremendously during the next few weeks. The doctors talked to me about giving David a weekend furlough to go home. They wanted someone that could be with him and maintain a diary of his daily activities. Mainly they wanted to see if he could safely be at home by himself if he was discharged to go home.

I was elated. I told the doctors that I would stay with him and monitor his activities. I was very excited because by now, David could remember nearly everything that I asked him to talk to me about. I asked him if he could remember his sister's phone number. He said no, but that he never had memorized it before. I got him his sister's phone number and he called her from the hospital and they visited on the phone for a few minutes. I was just so happy that he was getting to go to his house. I wanted him to get well.

I went home walking on cloud nine, knowing that he would be getting to come spend the weekend at home. This would help him remember more things that he may have forgotten due to the accident. I was trying so hard to keep him from having to be moved to Oklahoma. David belonged in Houston.

On the Saturday morning, I went to the rehab center to bring David home for the weekend. We received all kinds of instructions and we were on the way home. He saw his house as we turned the corner onto his street. He started to cry. He said he thought he would never get to come home. We walked up the stairs to the back door of his apartment. He unlocked the door and we walked in. He was very happy. We hugged and we both cried. He was home.

The weekend was uneventful. I took notes of what he did and if he remembered things and if he did activities safely. He remembered turning the stove on and safely used the stove, knives and walking up and down the stairs. He did great. We were both very happy. I was ecstatic. He was fine. He would be just fine.

On Sunday afternoon, we got ready to take David back to the rehab center. He did not mind going back because he said he would probably be discharged in a few days. And so he was.

CHAPTER 28

DAVID COMES HOME

David was finally discharged from the rehab center. He would have to continue rehab therapy on an outpatient basis. He was instructed on where to report for further therapy and we went home. On the way home, we drove by the location where he would continue his therapy. We also planned how we would get him to and from therapy and me not lose my job. David was not legally allowed to drive until his therapy was completed and the physician stated that David could be able to drive.

Once we got home we carried his few belongings inside and David walked inside his apartment, going through his mail and checking his refrigerator trying to figure out what he needed to buy at the grocery store. David was very happy to be home. And I was very happy that he was home, that he would be himself again, and that I would have my lovely friend back home where he belonged.

Since David was not able to handle his financial accounts or drive until after the doctor released him, he would borrow money from me for groceries and whatever else he needed. We settled into a routine of me driving him to therapy in the morning. When he was through with therapy at noon, I would pick him up, drive him home and then I would go back to work. I did this until he completed his therapy. Occasionally he would get a ride home with someone that he made friends with while getting physical therapy. That person lived close to where David lived and offered to drive David home,

Finally the day arrived when he completed his therapy and the paper work was completed so that he could get his driver's license back and he could get back to handling his own money. It took a few weeks, but he got everything changed. David felt lost at not being able to be in charge of his own finances and he did not like having to borrow money from me. Now he could handle his own money and drive his car. Things seemed to be back to normal again.

I continued working and David would come over to my apartment after I got home from work and we would talk. I would ask him what he had done during the day and he would say he had done nothing. I noticed he did not seem himself. He seemed somewhat quiet, pensive.

David and I continued our routine that we had prior to his accident. I would come home from work and then we would go out to eat. We both enjoyed eating and we both began to gain weight. David had lost a lot of weight from the time he was in the hospital. He was down to a size thirty six waist now. But we both enjoyed driving to an "all you can eat" restaurant and pigging out. On the way home we would talk about how we would start trying to lose weight. But next day, we would end up at a different "all you can eat" restaurant and pig out again. We were both happy.

David seemed to have changed since the accident. At first, I did not notice the change in him because I was so happy that he was fine and I had my beloved friend home again. But then I started noticing little things at first. David starting saving all the newspapers and junk mail that was being mailed to his address. He refused to dispose of any flyer or paper he had. I would ask him if I could clean his apartment and he would say his apartment was fine.

David had always taken good care of his personal hygiene. He would shower and change into clean clothes daily. I started noticing that he would go a couple of days without shaving or go all day without combing his hair. I would kid with him about getting to be lazy and we would both laugh, but then it became a regular thing.

David had always maintained his yard. But now he would not mow the grass and weeds had grown tall in the yard. I would do some yard work, weeding and what little else he would allow me to do. I bought my own lawn mower because he would not allow me to use his lawn mower. He would stop me from doing yard work if he saw me working in the yard. I would have to get angry with him in order for him to allow me to mow the grass.

Time went by and he continued being quiet but seemed to be okay from the injury. Then one day he said he wanted me to go with him to see his lawyer. He told me that he wanted to make changes to his will. He told me that he had talked with his sister and his young brother and had told them that he would be changing the will. He then told me that he wanted me to be the beneficiary of his estate. I asked him why he would want to do that. I told him that his sister and his brother were his family and that he should not change the will.

David looked at me and said, "Joe, you are my family. You and your children, Nelda, David, Jackie, your grand-children and Crystal, my great-granddaughter, you all are my family. Your family comes to see me. Your family in-vites me to their homes to eat. They give me presents at Christmas and on my birthdays. Any time Nelda fixes food, she invites me. You were there while I was in the hospital. You are my family." He started to cry. I told him that we would talk about it later.

By this time my daughter and her children had moved into the apartment downstairs, at David's insistence. He stated that he wanted to help my daughter Nelda and so he insisted that she move in downstairs. Also, David informed me that he did not want us to pay him rent. He just wanted us to pay for our own utility bills. I asked him why he was doing that and he again repeated to me that we were his family. He said he loved my family and that he cared for Chrystal. I tried to talk to David, insisting that we needed to pay rent, but once David made up his mind, he would refuse to discuss things any further.

I continued working in the nursing home. I was get-ting paid well, forty hour weeks, and worked from eight a.m. to five p.m., Monday through Friday. It was a good job for me, as far as I was concerned.

During this time, I would occasionally visit my Father and my sisters that lived in Brady. My Father was getting old and David felt that I should see my Father as much as I could. My oldest sister was looking after my Father. He lived alone in a government apartment where he and my mother had lived before she died. I used to visit him and sleep in the same twin bed my mother slept in. The bed was comfortable but the temperature was not. My Father liked to sleep with the window open and have the night breeze come in through the window. It would be hot for me. I would lay there sweating until I would fall asleep. I am glad that I did look after and help take care of both my parents.

CHAPTER 29

HANNA FINDS A HOME

One day during the month of September of 2001, David and I had gone out to eat and were on our way home. I asked if we could stop and see the dogs, since we were driving near the SPCA. He said that would be a great idea. But he warned me, "Joe, we are only going to look at the dogs. You cannot get a dog. You have to work and I do not want to have to take care of a dog." I told him I did not want a dog. I just wanted to look at the dogs.

Once inside we walked around looking at all the dogs they had in cages and making comments as to which ones were cute and which ones were not so cute. He went one direction and I went the other direction.

As I walked along the cages and looked at the little dogs, I came to a cage where a small reddish brown Chihuahua was sitting in the corner at the back of the cage. She was sitting there looking sad with her head hanging half way to the floor of the cage and her eyes looking up at me. She did not move or bark. She looked sad, lonely and was very quiet. I thought at first she may be sick.

I stood there for a minute staring at the little dog and she stared back, not moving and her head still hanging down and eyes looking upward towards me. I stuck one finger through one of the holes of the cage wire. Not moving her head, she moved her eyes to look at my finger and then moved her eyes back up to look at me. Then she very slowly stood up and slowly walked to the front of the cage and sat down leaning against my finger. I moved my finger sideways so that I could touch her and attempted to pet her. Then I removed my finger.

After I removed my finger, she turned her head and raised her eyes to look at me. Then she slowly stood up and slowly walked back to the same little corner of the cage and sat down. Again, with her head hanging halfway to the floor of the cage as she had been before, she raised her eyes upward looking at me. She never made a sound.

I thought that was neat. I liked that. Then I did the same thing again, sticking my finger through the cage wire and she did the same thing again. This time I touched her head and her ears and talked to her as if I was talking to a child. I petted her head and touched her back in a petting motion as much as I could through the cage wire. I pulled my fingers back out and she again stood up and walked back to the corner of the cage.

I called out to David to come and see. When he came over, I showed him how the dog would come over and most importantly, how she looked at me. David looked and he liked it also but he said, "No, you cannot have a dog, Joe.

Remember what I told you on the way here." I agreed that I remembered what we had talked about.

As we started to walk away from the cage, I stopped and said, "David, I want the dog." David turned and looked at me. I repeated, "I want that dog." David asked, "Joe, are you serious?" "Yes.", I answered, "I want this dog."

David called the lady that had been talking to him earlier as I walked to the cage where the little dog was. Pointing at me he told the lady I wanted to see the dog. She got the dog out of the cage and took us into a small room and closed the door. She sat the small dog on the middle of the long bench in the small room. As the attendant said, this was to see if the dog and I would bond.

I sat on one end of the bench and David sat on the other end. The little dog quickly walked over to me, crawled on my leg and lay down on my lap. She laid there with her eyes closed. It was love at first sight. I could not leave this little dog here. She had to come home with me now, today. David and I had fallen in love with the dog instantly.

The attendant came back and asked what we thought about the dog. David told her I wanted to take the dog with me. We were sent to the office to do the paper work, pay and bring her home. When I got to the front desk, I explained to the young lady that I wanted to complete the paper work to adopt the dog. She explained that I had to have permission from my landlord, in writing, that I could have the dog in my apartment. Then David explained that he was my landlord and that he was giving his permission for me to have the dog in the apartment. It ended up that the only way that I could bring my little dog home was for David to adopt her. He did that and all three of us went home.

David had owned a Chihuahua a few years ago that was the same color as this one. I asked David if I could use his dog's name for my own dog. He was very pleased about that. On the way home David said he wanted to stop and buy our new dog some bones, food, and bowls that she could eat from.

So Hanna became our beautiful loving, little dog. I do not know in what way she had been abused, but I knew I would protect her and never let any harm come to her. The SPCA had said she was two years old, but she grew after we brought her home. She got up to fourteen pounds and she did not look fat. She looked good for her size.

David helped me take care of Hanna, since he was home all day and I had to work. He enjoyed helping take care of Hanna. I would bring her over to his apartment before I went to work and he would bring her to me after I got home from work. She loved David but she knew I was her master. When David and I were in the same apartment or room, Hanna would follow me or sit in my lap instead of his. David used to say, "That's the way it's supposed to be. You are her master."

CHAPTER 30

LOSS OF MY FATHER

In October, my older sister called me to let me know that my Father was in the hospital. I told David that I was going to see my Father and David told me he would go with me to help me drive. Hanna came with us.

I got to the hospital and went in to see my Father. He looked good for a ninety year old man. He was still very alert mentally, and we visited off and on that day. David had stayed at my sister's home to take care of Hanna.

My Father had previously had two heart attacks and survived them both. Now he was having trouble with his heart again and also high blood pressure. He never had problems with confusion and very little forgetfulness. My older sister had been taking care of him but had mentioned she was tired. My Father was a stubborn man. Once he decided on something, it was difficult to change his mind or to get him to do what he needed to do to stay in good health.

I had talked with my older sister about placing my Father in a nursing home. He had fallen a few times at home and my older sister had to get someone to come and help him get up. I felt that it was not safe for him to be living by himself. My older sister did not want to place my Father in a nursing home and had difficulty with the thought of doing that, but she finally decided to do it.

The physician told us that my Father was doing well enough to be sent to the nursing home in a couple of days. So I decided to go back to Houston. It is a long and tiring drive from Brady to Houston. I hated the long drive back to Houston but with David also driving it was a big help. I did make the long drive by myself on several occasions, but I always dreaded the long drive.

I went to work the next day after we got back from Brady. Two days after I had gotten back from seeing my Father, my older sister called to let me know that my Father would be discharged from the hospital that after- noon and be taken straight to the nursing home. He ar- rived at the nursing home in the late afternoon. He was not happy about having to be in the nursing home, but there was no other choice.

Very early the next morning my older sister called me to let me know my Father had passed away. I was getting ready to go to work when I received the phone call and so I called my administrator at work and told her about my Father's death. I called David then I drove the long way back to Brady by myself.

My sister informed me that my Father had been doing fine through the night and was doing fine when they got him ready for breakfast. The nurse had sat him up in a chair beside the bed and had gone to get him his breakfast tray. When she came back with the breakfast tray, my Father was gone. It was that fast. He did not suffer or linger on for days in pain. We were grateful for that.

While my Father was in the hospital, my older sister and I had come in the morning to be with him. When we got to his room, he asked me if I had talked with my Mother. My Mother had passed away at least fourteen or fifteen years earlier. I told him no, I had not seen or talked with her. He repeated that my Mother had just left and if I hurried down the hall I could probably catch up with her. I told him I would do that later. Another morning when we got there, he asked my sister and I if we had seen Jose, his older brother, who had just left. Jose had been there visiting with him. Jose had passed away before my Mother. I told my sister that this was not a good sign. I had heard that somewhere.

My Father died a few days later. Is that coincidence? I am not superstitious, but in my line of work, you hear about things occurring that perhaps are hard to explain or understand how and why they occurred as they did.

I am not sure how I felt about my Father dying. My Father and I had not been close. My Father did not treat me like other fathers treated their sons. Or maybe, he did not treat me the way I wanted him to treat me. My Father had not taken time to play with me or to teach me to do things that I felt my Father should have taught me. For example, he did not teach me things like how to fix a flat, change the oil in the car, cut down trees, or build chicken coops. My Mother was the one that would teach me to do those things. I think I loved my Father but I am not sure.

I know he showed more love towards my daughter and some of his other grandchildren than he ever did towards me. I want to think that he loved me and that is the way it shall be.

My three sisters and I went to make the funeral arrangements. I allowed my sisters to choose the casket and make whatever arrangements they felt they needed to make and I paid for all the costs. David had told me to make the funeral arrangements and then let him know how much money to transfer from my savings account to my checking account to pay for the funeral. And I did just that.

My children arrived at the funeral home. The funeral director had allowed the family to view the body before the body was open for the public to view. My Father looked just as he had always looked. He never seemed to have aged.

The funeral was held in Melvin, his body taken to the Melvin Catholic church and then to the cemetery where he was buried alongside my Mother. They had celebrated their 50th wedding anniversary and now they would be together for always. My Mother would be happy now. Now, they were together.

I came back to Houston about two days after the funeral. On my way back, I thought about my Father and realized that I knew very little about him, his family or his past. What little I knew was what my Mother had told us about him. When we would ask him about his family or things about his past or his growing-up years, he would just say we were crazy.

Now it was just my three sisters and me, left to carry on our parent's legacy. My parents were poor, so there was no money or wealth to pass on down to us children. But my Mother taught us to love and to respect others. My Mother always gave so much love to us, her children, her grandchildren and her friends. My Mother taught me that I could do whatever I wanted to do for myself, for my future, and my career. She would always encourage me when my Father would discourage me. She was a very positive thinker. She would say to me, "You can do it if you set your mind to it."

My Mother had always treasured her friendships. She felt that friends were very important. She showed respect towards her friends and enjoyed the visits with her friends. I learned from her to love and respect my friends. To this day I thoroughly enjoy my visits with my friends and I can remember specific things about each one of my friends. That is the legacy that my Mother passed on to me and that I want to pass on to my children, grandchildren and so on.

CHAPTER 31

MY BUSINESS VENTURE

Time went by and David and I continued on our same routine. I worked, signed my paycheck over to him and he would deposit the money in the bank. I did not have to work extra hours as I used to, but every time I would tell David that I could take care of my own finances now, he would insist that he continue to do so because it was no trouble to him. I let him continue taking care of my finances because I could see he enjoyed doing that. He

enjoyed telling me how much I had saved, interest earned and then he would tell me how much I will have saved by a certain time in the future at that rate. It pleased him greatly to do that for me.

In April 2004, I decided to start my own consulting business for home health agencies. I had learned about home health when I owned my own home health agency but also by working as a state surveyor. I learned how to survey home health agencies and used that information to assist home health agencies maintain compliance with Federal and State regulations.

When I first told David what I wanted to do, he was not too keen on the idea. He was afraid I might not do well with the business. But the more we talked about it, the more he felt that I could at least give it a try. It was scary for me also, but I felt I could do a good job. I knew the Federal and State regulations for home health and I could learn whatever else I did not know.

David and I decided I would start my business working from my apartment. He and I consulted with our accountant and my lawyer. My lawyer helped us complete the paper work to name the business and do whatever other paper work needed to be done. David helped a lot with setting up the systems that I would use to maintain the records that pertained to payables and money that was earned. I could see that he enjoyed setting up business files and he would explain to me how the receivables and payables process would be done. He spent hours setting up files and ledgers. David refused to use computers and so he kept all records on paper. He would not even let me pay one single bill from on-line. I went along with whatever he wanted to do since I felt he had the knowledge and experience with accounting.

David would come to my apartment early in the mornings and while he would be setting up files, I would work on the other aspect of the business. I had to write policies and procedures for the home health agencies that I would be working with. I had already written a set of policies before, so I knew what I had to do for this agency. Once I wrote the policies I had them copy righted. I created all kinds of forms to use and really enjoyed doing all the hard work in getting the business all set up. David seemed to enjoy working long hours helping me. I told him I needed to pay him and he said, "Absolutely not. I want to help you and I enjoy helping you. I don't want any money." I hated not paying him, but I had also learned that I could not push David. Once he set his mind on something that was it. Nothing would change his mind.

David and I had planned on my business to take a few months to start getting clients. We were not prepared for how quickly the company grew. About two weeks after I decided to start my own business, I started getting calls from people wanting me to help them with their current business or helping them start a new business. My business grew quickly. With David helping me and both of us working long hours, we could not keep up with the paper work. I had completed the policies and the agencies wanted to buy my policies. I could not work fast enough to keep up with the demands. I had to go to their place of business, review their policies and clinical records and then type the reports. David and I worked on the policy manuals at night.

After a few weeks of long work days, David suggested I get someone to help out, at least part time. I hired Ashley, my granddaughter. David and Ashley would be at home working while I went to the agencies to do the reviews. It was going really well except for one thing. My clients would call at all hours of the night to leave messages and fax forms. Every time the fax machine started printing, my Hanna would start barking. I could not get a good night's sleep. Also, I did not want my clients to come to my house. Some of my clients would want to just come by and talk to me. I would have to meet them at another place that we would agree on. David finally said I should try to find a small office for me to work from.

Our next door neighbor and her friend worked in real estate and she helped me find a one room office about one mile from where I lived. The rent was very reasonable so I rented the office space. The office was very convenient for both David and me. I continued doing very well getting clients and of course, that meant more business. I finally had to contract with a friend to help in the office. He was very good at working with people and so he and I did very well.

David continued taking care of the financial part of the business. He kept excellent records and it was very easy taking care of my taxes. Our accountant and David had worked together at one time, so they would have a good time visiting and laughing each time we went to our accountant's office to take care of the business taxes. They had a good time visiting. I had to remind David about not visiting on my time. He would laugh at me. The visits were really not that long and I really did not mind paying for them to visit.

My work was going really great and I was busy and David was busy. But David was not taking care of his health. He enjoyed eating. He and I used to go eat at different restaurants and we used to enjoy eating, usually a lot. We both began to gain weight. I talked with David and decided that I did not want to gain any more weight. I stopped going to the "all you can eat" places we used to go. But David continued going by himself.

David had lost weight when he had been at the hospital. He had gotten down to a thirty six waist. He looked good and of course, it was healthy for him. But then he started eating. It seemed as if he could not stop eating. He slowly started gaining weight.

David also did not exercise at all. He walked Hanna several times a day, but other than that, he would not do anything else as far as activity. The work that he did for my business did not require much physical activity. So he kept gaining weight.

David was my dearest friend and I did not want him to get sick. I used to tell him that I needed him to stay healthy because he was my work partner. I would tell him that I could not run the business without him. He would only laugh and say, "Joe, you can do anything you set your mind to do. You have enough courage to start a business on your own. You are not scared of doing that. I would never have had the courage to do what you have done." I would tell him that I got the courage because I had him by my side. If he was not by my side, I would not do it alone.

But he continued eating. And he gained the weight. His health was not good at all. His lower legs were swollen. His legs began to weep through the skin from being swollen so big. His skin became dry and scaly. The doctor had prescribe treatment to his legs and recommended a skin specialist. The treatment to his legs was to be performed twice a day. I did his treatments twice a day, applied the medication and wrapped his legs with the dressings. I reminded him about the skin specialist but David said that he would call the skin specialist when he was ready to call him.

David continued taking care of the financial aspect of the consulting business. I could see that he really enjoyed doing that. Each time I talked to him about letting me take care of the finances, he would remind me that I was too busy doing the consulting with the agencies and did not have the time to take care of the finances. "Besides," he would say, "you do not know anything about finances. You need to let me do it." So I let him continue taking care of the finances. I had watched him and noted how he managed the finances, kept the records and how he documented all payables, deposits, and kept receipts. David was very meticulous and very precise about keeping records. He was very good at what he did.

My consulting business kept growing. I had clients in several parts of the state. I flew to other cities to consult with the home health agencies and assist them in whatever way I could. I enjoyed my work and I really cared about my clients. I wanted to do whatever I could to help them be in compliance with the Medicare and State regulations. I was willing to do extras for the clients without pay.

David and I kept eating out together in the evenings and twice on weekends. Sometimes I would eat while at work or eat with friends, so I would call him to see if he wanted me to bring something for him to eat. He always appreciated that.

But David kept gaining weight and his health was not improving. His breathing became heavy with any activity and at times he would be gasping for breath. He began sleeping in the recliner in my apartment because he could not breathe well if he lay down. I tried to get him to go to the doctor but he refused, saying that there was nothing wrong with him. He would say emphatically, "Joe, I am fine. Stop worrying about me."

But I could not stop worrying. My dearest friend was not doing well and I had no way of helping him. He would not let me help him. And I did not know how to get him to understand that he needed help. I would tell him how much I cared, how much it was hurting me to see him gasping for breath, seeing his legs getting so much worse.

David had gotten to where he was not letting me do the treatment to his legs. I had to get upset with him in order for him to let me treat his legs. His legs were draining constantly. I would go to the dollar store and buy floor mats to place on the floor in front of the recliner he sat in.

The fluid from his legs would drain to the floor mat and the floor mat would protect the carpet.

Sometimes I would cry when treating his legs because they looked so bad. He insisted that his legs did not hurt. Sometimes dried skin would fall off when I treated his legs. I felt so helpless in trying to help him. Sometimes I would threaten him by telling him that I was going to call his sister or his younger brother so that they could come and force him to see a doctor. He would become very upset and I had to give him my word that I would never do that.

As I have said before, David was the most honest man I have ever known. I trusted him with my life. And if David told you he would do something for you, you could rest assured that he would do that something. David kept his word. And he trusted me. I never wanted to do anything that would break his trust in me. But I did find out that when I threatened to call his family, he would allow me to do the treatments. He caught on very quickly as to what I was doing and he let me know that he knew. We would both laugh about it, but he would let me do the treatments.

But by now he needed much more medical care to his legs than the treatments were providing. The scaly, broken skin areas were all the way from his knees to his feet. The blue jeans he wore would get wet from the draining fluid from his legs. He wore blue jeans to cover his legs.

Besides ignoring his health, David had completely lost any desire to keep his apartment clean. He kept every piece of junk mail that was sent to him. He would not throw anything away. He started piling newspapers on the floor in every room of his apartment.Dishes were piled in the kitchen sink. David had never been like this before. He did not dust often, but he was very meticulous about the kitchen. His sister used to come visit him before the accident and she would dust his apartment for him. He used to say that he hated for her to come and work dusting his apartment but he appreciated what she did and I think she enjoyed doing that for him.

But now she had not visited in some time and he kept hoarding papers. I knew that David was not in good health. And he knew it too. He would talk about how I should do things once he was gone. I would always tell him that he was not going anywhere. I knew what he was talking about, but it always seems to be hard for people to talk about death. Being a nurse, I had dealt with death many times and even pronounced patients when I had to. But it still is not easy talking about losing someone you love.

One day I came home from work and David was waiting for me in my apartment. He wanted to talk to me about his estate. He wanted me to have the house. I told him that his sister wanted the house and he needed to leave the house to her. Again he informed me that he had already talked with his sister and brother and that he had informed them of such.

At this time we both agreed on the medical power of attorney. We sat down with my daughter and I spoke to my son. I told them that David would have medical power of attorney over me and I would have medical power of attorney over him. We went to the lawyer and the lawyer completed the paper work for medical power of attorney. We both signed. We continued disagreeing on his estate. I told him to leave the house to his sister. I told him that I cared about him and about his health. That was the most important thing to me. The argument was not settled, but we decided to leave it until a later time.

David had great difficulty walking and moving around. I worried about him constantly. If I called and he did not answer or if he did not call me back after a few minutes, I would become worried. I would wonder why he did not answer the phone. If he went grocery shopping, I would worry about him. He always went grocery shopping late in the evening.

I got him a cell phone. I felt more at ease if he had a phone with him in case he needed help. At one time he had fallen in the parking lot of the grocery store and he could not stand up. Two men walking by helped him to stand up. Another time he fell outside the veterinary's office. He and I had met there to get Hanna to the veterinary. David had told me to go on back to work, that he would go back home. After I left, he said he missed the step in front of the veterinary's office and fell. A young man standing nearby tried to help him but could not get him up on his feet. The young man had to seek help from another young man to help David to his feet.

After I got David the cell phone, I was able to call him and he could answer almost right away. I was more at ease. Occasionally, he would forget his cell phone and if I called and he did not answer, I would leave work and check on him. He would get upset that I had left work to check on him, but I would always tell him, if he answered the phone like he was expected to, I would not have to come home and check on him.

David continued taking care of my finances, both personal and business. I tried to take over my own finances, but he told me, "Joe, I have nothing else to do. If you don't let me take care of your financial business, I won't have anything to do." It made me feel really bad. I never again tried to take that job away from him. He seemed to enjoy coming to the office, sitting at his desk and documenting on the records. He had his own shelf where he kept his small calculator that he got at the dollar store, mechanical pencils that he preferred over regular pencils, and a few other odds and ends that he kept. From the office he would go to the bank, take care of the banking for me and then go home. He became friends with a lady cashier at the bank and he would always prefer to have her assist him.

David would come with me to my children's parties, family get-togethers or any other family gatherings my children had. He got a lot of pleasure when my oldest great-granddaughter would run to him and hug his leg. He would then pick her up and carry her. Later she got too big for him to carry her, but she would still hug him.

My life was a routine. I would work long hours Monday through Friday, come home, we would eat and then I would go walking and then go to bed. I would bring my laptop computer and do work at home most of the time. David would stay in my apartment and watch television and sleep.

My work kept me very busy. I kept consulting with the home health agencies, providing classes for the administrators as required by the state, and assisting others with starting their home health businesses. David kept coming to the office to complete his documentation for the business finances. I offered to bring the data to him at home, but he insisted on coming to the office.

My business office was on the second floor of the building and he had to struggle to climb the stairs to the second floor. By the time he got to the top of the stairs, he would be breathing very hard, gasping for breath. It hurt me deeply to hear him gasp for breath and to see him struggle to walk.

His feet were so swollen. He could only wear slip-on shoes because he could not find shoes that he could get his feet into. I bought him a pair of leather slip-on shoes that he liked. I took the pair of slip-on shoes to the shoe repair shop so that they could add an inch of elastic at the center top part of the sandal. When he put his feet into the sandals, the elastic would stretch and the sandals would fit perfectly. He was very pleased when I brought him the sandals. He could wear them comfortably and he had something to wear on his feet. In cold weather, I made sure he wore socks to help keep his feet warm.

It started happening occasionally and slowly progressed. David started having accidents, wetting his clothes. The first time it happened, he was very upset and embarrassed. He kept apologizing for wetting his clothes in my apartment. I went to his apartment to get him some clean clothes and assisted him with taking a shower. I kept trying to make him understand that I felt bad for him but that I was here to help him.

David's physical condition kept getting worse. He walked slowly due to his extreme weight. I had to buy him larger sized clothes as he kept gaining weight. He had gotten up to weighing three hundred pounds, then three hundred fifty pounds, but I could not get him to do anything about his eating. He simply loved to eat and refused to make any efforts at controlling his eating.

I do not cook. I hated the thought of having to learn to cook. I ate out a lot. When I ate at home, I ate very simple, easy-to-put-together meals, for example, tuna out of a can on a slice of bread or a slice of lunch meat between two slices of bread. I hate having to use mustard or mayonnaise, lettuce and tomatoes. I feel that if I use all those extras, I will get too close to cooking. I guess lazy is a good word to use. When I went to the grocery store, I usually bought different kinds of chips, ice cream, canned tuna, bread and lunch meat.

David would come to my apartment and would eat with me. He did not mind eating the sandwiches the way I prepared them. He felt the sandwiches were fine the way I fixed them. He would ask me to fix him a sandwich while he watched television. Sometimes I would cook a meal like my Mother used to cook, ground beef with canned tomatoes and different spices. Or I would boil some chicken legs in water with spices. I would remove the skin when I boiled the chicken legs and sometimes I would add fresh vegetables. And that is the extent of my cooking.

I got very busy with my consulting business and David kept on with maintaining the financial documentation. My home health consulting business was doing well and I spent many hours in my office doing research work so that I could better assist the agencies. I found it very interesting reading about state and Medicare regulations and changes to the regulations. As strange as it may sound, I enjoyed reading policy and procedure manuals.

I had gotten approved by the state to teach state required administrative classes that would provide continued education hours for administrators and assistant administrators of home health agencies. I found that I enjoyed teaching the classes. I enjoyed doing whatever work was needed to assist the agencies maintain compliance with state and Medicare regulations.

The state required administrators and directors of nurses of home health agencies to attend certain classes prior to starting their agency. My classes that I taught were approved by the state and it provided continued education contact hours.

One very memorable time that I enjoyed helping start a home health business was when I met two pretty women who came to talk to me about starting their own home health agency.

On the day of the class I had twenty five administrators and registered nurses registered for the class. But the two pretty women that were scheduled to attend had not shown up for the class. I started the class. Just as I had started the class, in walked the two pretty ladies. Usually, when people walk in late to a class, they try to be very quiet and not disturb the class or draw attention.

These ladies walked in apologizing for being late and talking about how bad the traffic was and asking if they had missed much of the class. Finally they were settled down and I started the class, again.

Lunch break was from 12 to 1pm and everyone was back in the classroom ready to start, except the two pretty ladies. I decided that I would let the class decide what day they wanted the second part of the class to be held. They chose a Friday and the date. Then the pretty ladies walked in.

I informed the two ladies of the day and date of the second class, and one of the ladies asked, "Could we change that day to some other day? I am flying to London to celebrate my birthday." I thought, how cute. I said no.

Much later after they had started their agency, I went to review their agency records to help them maintain compliance with Medicare and the state. After completing my review of their agency records, I sat with the two of them in the administrator's office to give them a report. One of the ladies was the administrator and the other was the director of nurses. They each sat on opposite sides of the desk and I sat at the one end of the desk. I started my report.

On the very first item I mentioned as a potential problem, the lady who was the administrator asked the nurse why there was a problem. The nurse answered and then the administrator responded and then the nurse answered and soon there was a shouting match. The administrator stood up with her hands on the desk and the nurse stood up on the other side of the desk, with their faces a few inches apart, yelling loudly at each other and banging on the desk with their closed fists. I thought to myself that I was about to be witness to a murder and I did not want to get involved.

I kept trying to calm them down but they could not hear me. After several minutes, the nurse lifts her open hand in a gesture with her finger nails facing the administrator. All of sudden the administrator takes a deep breath and says, "Your nails, they are beautiful. Where did you have them done?" The nurse says "Oh baby, didn't I tell you I found this place where I had them done? I thought I had told you. I am sorry." Then they called the other ladies who worked in the office to show them the nails. I thought, what is going on? I was confused. I had never seen anything like this before.

The arguing continued through each item that we discussed until I was through with the report. As I walked to the car I thought about what had happened. Through all their arguing they still have remained best of friends. I thought to myself as I got in my car, I love these ladies. And I still do.

But I also encountered those persons that were not interested in running business according to the state and Medicare regulations. Some persons thought that starting a home health agency would be a road to quick financial gains. As more persons became more careless about the way their home health agency business was managed, it became harder for me to enjoy conducting business with them.

Medicare began making more changes, thus making it more difficult for home health agencies to be started and for some agencies to continue in the business. I personally feel that our government does a lot of stupid things. The way they ran home health is one of those stupid things. The changes that Medicare made are for the better, but as they say, they closed the gates after the horses were gone.

David began to see that I was having a difficult time with some of my clients. They did not want to pay. Some of my clients consistently and persistently would ask for discounts. They stated since they would be sending me a lot of clients, I should give them a great discount. Yea, right. I would tell some of them not to insult me by asking me to lower my prices. I was already the least expensive consultant by my choice.

I continued with my home health consulting business because I enjoyed what I did. I had clients that were the nicest people and easy to work for. They appreciated the help that I provided to them. They were the ones I wanted to help the most.

Time goes by very fast. My grandchildren grew older and of course, that means so did I. I had friends who were very nice, good friends, but I did not go out very much. I dedicated my life to working. I was very concerned about David's health and I made it a point to call him very often during the day and I stayed home as much as I could to make sure he would be okay.

David seemed to be gaining more weight and his mobility was very slow and unsteady. I was always checking in on him if he did not come over to my apartment when I was home. He would tell me not to worry about him but I just could not keep from worrying.

David and I had been very close friends for a long time now and he was a very important part of my life. I saw that he was having difficulty breathing and getting about physically and I wanted to be there for him in whatever his need.

The frequency for David to have accidents before he could get to the bathroom had increased. We both felt badly about his accidents but he could not help it. I would help him change clothes and assure him that I did not mind helping him. David would always apologize and I knew it made him feel bad and I would reassure him it was okay. I would tell him not to apologize but he would do it every time.

David would always apologize if he felt he had said or done something that would bother me. For example, he always went with me so that I could buy clothes, such as jeans, underwear or scrubs for work. I would explain to him what I was looking for and we would go different directions to look for clothes. Suddenly I would hear him call out loud in the store so that all the other people could hear, "Joe, what size do you wear? Is it forty or forty-two?" It would be embarrassing to see people looking at me. If I did not look towards him, he would ask again, except louder. Once a lady said to me pointing towards David, "I think that man is calling you." Embarrassed because people were listening to us, I would say out loud, "Extra small." Sometimes I would tell him before we got to the stores to not call out loud and let the world know I was fat. He would apologize and I could tell he really felt badly about embarrassing me in front of people. The sweet thing about it though, he really was trying to help me and did it innocently. He never would have wanted to embarrass me in public. He was too caring for that.

David and I would spend a lot of time in my apartment talking. I would tell him about my work, what I had done and ask for his advice on certain things. We always found things to talk about from the past.

David would tell me how he lost his father and his mother. In fact, David talked about his parents quite often. His mother had died from cancer. He always talked about how he would try to go on weekends to go see his mother. He always felt he had not made a good enough effort to go see her during the time she was sick. Prior to his mother getting sick, he would tell me his mother would come to stay with him for a few days. David would tell me how his mother had gotten his little Chihuahua trained to climb the stairs at his house. He remembered how the little dog looked trying to climb the stairs and then finally climbing one step at a time.

He would also tell me about the time he and his younger brother were walking home from school and his younger brother got into a fight with another little boy. David would often cry because he said he did not know how to fight and defend or protect his little brother. He would sometimes laugh because he said all he could think of saying was, "You better come on home. Mother will be upset if we get home late."

David and I laughed about the funny things that had happened to us in the past. He would ask me questions about my past, my family, and I would ask him questions about his past. We both often laughed and cried together when we talked about our pasts.

CHAPTER 32

A SPECIAL PERSON IN MY LIFE

David kept encouraging me to go out with my friends. I would go with friends but not too often. He, on two or three occasions, told me that he wanted me to meet someone that I could care for and maybe someday to share my life with. I always made excuses why I did not want to meet someone, but the truth was, nobody ever seemed interested in me enough to want to talk to me. I was shy and quiet and it was not easy for me to strike up a conversation with anyone. I just did not know what to say. I did not drink alcohol so I had no reason to go to bars.

I belonged to a senior's group here in Houston and I would go to their monthly pot luck parties. But I never seemed to meet anyone or at least converse with someone. I would go home and watch TV with David.

One day, Rudy, a friend of mine, invited me to a Sunday brunch being held at a Mexican restaurant in the Montrose area where I lived. Another friend came and picked me up and we went to the brunch. There was a large group and I sat directly across from Rudy and Paul. Rudy and Paul had been partners and living together for over thirty years. Rudy told me that a new member of the group would be sitting next to him and he was responsible for introducing the new member to others in the group.

When the new member came over to sit next to Rudy, I took notice. He was nice looking and very friendly. We were introduced and I think I spoke to the new member. I was trying to think of something to talk to him about and the more I thought, the more my mind would go blank. This still happens to me when I am around people I do not know. So I said nothing. Finally people from our group were starting to leave. I wanted to get to know the new member, but I did not know what to say. People had gotten up and were walking around visiting with each other. I got up and walked to the side of the table where the new member was still sitting talking to others. I sat next to him still trying to think of something to say to him. I said nothing.

On the way home, I asked my friend who had taken me to the brunch if he thought that the new member was nice. My friend said yes. I said I did too. My friend dropped me off at home and I went inside. David was there with Hanna and I was happily greeted by Hanna with her jumping onto my lap as I sat down. After I told David about the brunch, I told him about the new member of the group. I told him his name was George and that I thought he was very nice and handsome. David asked me if I had talked to him. I said no, I did not know what to say. We watched TV for a while and then I changed clothes and went to the office to work for a while.

I kept thinking about the new member and wondered how I could get to talk to him. I called Rudy and told him I liked the new member and I was disappointed I had not talked to him. Rudy told me to give him a call. Rudy said he would give me the new member's phone number and I could call him. I told Rudy I could not call the new member because I did not know what to say to him. Rudy then told me, "Email him." And so I did. I invited him to a birthday party I had been invited to and he accepted. We went to the party and then made plans to go out to eat that weekend.

I told David about George and David was happy for me. He said he wanted to get to meet George. I had also told George about David and that I wanted him to meet David. After they met, David told me that George seemed very nice, friendly and genuine.

George and I got to know each other better and our relationship became more serious. I told David about my feelings towards George and he was happy for me. I still spent a lot of time with David. George would come over and the three of us would visit.

CHAPTER 33

MY DEAREST FRIEND IS GONE

One day, about a year after I had met George, David and I were sitting in my apartment visiting and watching television. David then told me that he was very happy that I had met George and that he felt George would take good care of me. I told David that George and I would take care of each other but that I would also continue caring for him, David, as long as I was able to. David then told me that would not be necessary, that he wanted me to be happy, and that he was at peace with knowing I had someone that would take care of me. He then told me that he loved me, thanked me for being there for him when he needed me and he wanted me to take good care of myself. I told him I loved him too and told him I could not have accomplished the things that I had done without him. He then told me he knew I would take good care of Hanna. He said that he had raised several dogs but he loved Hanna the most. He then looked at Hanna and he said, "She is so beautiful. She is a precious little girl.' I agreed with him.

I began to feel uncomfortable with the conversation. I did not like what David was saying and I immediately changed the subject and got up to do something, anything but continue with the conversation. I looked at David sitting in my recliner he always sat in when he came to visit. I loved my dearest friend. He meant so much to me.

He was watching television and nodding fighting to stay awake. He always did that until he would finally fall asleep. I would always let him sleep as long as he wanted. If it was cold, I would cover him with a blanket to make sure he was not cold.

That evening, Saturday March the 28th, George prepared supper and baked a cake for the three of us. We all three ate and visited while we ate. David had a big smile on his face when I brought the tray with food George had prepared. As I have said, David enjoyed eating. His face would brighten up and a big smile would form on his face.

After we finished eating George and I cleaned the kitchen and David asked us if we would finish watching the movie with him. The movie was "Ben Hur". We both sat down and watched the movie with him. During the movie, David would cry during certain scenes, like when Jesus was carrying the cross and fell and when Charlton Heston gave Him water to drink, and during the time in the cave when Heston's mother and sister got cured from the leprosy.

After the movie, George and I went to George's apartment to spend the night. David said he would take Hanna walking and then go home to his apartment. George and I left and I called David before I went to sleep. He was still in my apartment watching television. We said good night and I hung up.

Part of our weekend routine was George and I would go to church at the nine o'clock service and then go eat. On the way to church, I called David to check on him. I called his mobile phone, then his apartment phone and then my apartment phone. I did not get an answer, but that was not very unusual. I told George I would call again after worship service.

After worship service I called David again as soon as I got in the car. I did not get an answer from any of the telephone numbers I called. I then called my daughter to go to David's apartment and see if he was there. I also told her to go to my apartment if he did not answer at his apartment. A few minutes later my daughter called me back. She could hear Hanna barking in my apartment but David was not answering the door. I told George to drive me home.

The drive home from church was not but a few minutes, but it seemed like forever. When we got to the driveway of the house, I quickly got out of the car and ran up the stairs. I was frantic. Horrible thoughts were going through my mind and I did not want to think. I wanted my mind to not be able to think.

As soon as I unlocked the door, I ran in and looked towards the recliner where David always sat. David was sitting there, with his head turned sideways just as he had always done when he had fallen asleep in the recliner. Only this time he was not asleep. I called out to him, but there was no answer. There was no breathing, His face was cold. His hands were cold. My most wonderful, dearest friend was gone. There was no response, just stillness.

My David had gone and I was not there with him. I felt so much hurt. Physical pain can be relieved by drugs, but there is nothing that can relieve the hurt that one feels when you lose someone you love. The loss and the loneliness completely engulf you, placing you somewhere between reality and a state of numbness. The reality was I realized that David was gone and we would never talk again. We would never laugh again or cry as we often did. There was nothing but the silence and the numbness I felt. It was all a bad dream and I was watching everything that was happening from somewhere else.

I know I called 911, or maybe someone else did, and the emergency medical people were there and so were the police. I cannot tell you who all was there but I remember one of the emergency medical persons telling me he was sorry but David was gone. After that a lot of questions to get the information they all needed.

I called David's nephew, his younger brother's son, to inform him and asked him to let his father know about David. I did just as David had instructed me to. David had previously told me that he wanted his nephew notified first in case anything happened to him. David's younger brother called me a few minutes later.

Funeral arrangements were made and my children, grandchildren, George and I drove to Oklahoma for the funeral. After the funeral we drove back to Houston.

I had met David in March, 1980 and I lost him in March of 2009. The time had gone by so fast. It did not seem like twenty-nine years had gone by. I have so many beautiful memories and I learned so much from David. He was always there for me.

The thing that hurt the most when David died was that I was not there at his side. He died alone. I never wanted him to die without me being at his side. He had always said that the thing that bothered him the most was that he would die alone. I felt very guilty because I was not there by his side. I used to tell him that I was going to die first because I did not want to feel the pain of losing him. It did not work out that way. And I feel the pain.

Even though I had my family with me and George was there with me and for me, I felt alone and lost. I felt like as if I was all by myself and all was just gone, lost.

I loved my parents dearly and I remember the pain I felt when they died. But the pain I felt with David's death was much more intense, different than what I felt for my parents. David had helped me to believe in myself, that I could accomplish and that I could be successful. He encouraged me. Lord, I wanted David back. I needed David to talk to me, to teach me math, fractions, and whatever we used to talk about. But I did not have David anymore and I had to go on. I would think to myself of what David would always say to me, "Joe, you can do whatever you set your mind to do." Now without David, I had to believe in that and remember and do what David had taught me. Hanna and I could and would make it.

CHAPTER 34

MY NEW LIFE

As I had mentioned, after the funeral we drove back home to Houston. I went back to work. George and I talked and we decided that I would move in with him. George and I had known each other a year now and we both felt we should live together. I still had Hanna and the poor little thing felt so lost. She had no idea what was going on, but she knew everything had changed for her and she acted frightened. I guess we both felt the same.

George was very nice, considerate and caring towards both Hanna and me. George had never really had a dog before and I was not sure how it would work out between Hanna and him.

George and I started our lives together on a routine schedule. George would go to work and I would take Hanna to the doggie day care and then go to work. I would pick her up after I got off work. I would get home before George and would try to start dinner. I did not and do not cook, so starting dinner means setting the table and getting the drinks. I would feed Hanna while George prepared dinner.

Hanna had been used to sleeping with me in my bed but I wanted her to sleep in her cage. She did not want to do that. She would get up on the sofa which we both did not want her to do. She also started having accidents in the apartment. I began to realize things were not working well with us. George never complained but I was afraid he would eventually get tired and kick us out. When I voiced my fears to George, he reassured me that Hanna and I were fine there with him.

Our apartment was on the fourth floor of the apartment complex so Hanna and I would walk down the stairs so she could go potty, then we would walk up the four flights of stairs to the apartment. Hanna would walk down the stairs but she would not walk up the stairs. I had to carry her up. She was not heavy, but I just wondered why she would not walk up the stairs. She used to when we lived at David's. But whatever reason, taking her potty was very good exercise for me.

Because the apartment was small for us, we decided to buy a house. We both felt we loved and cared enough for each other that we wanted to buy a house together. So we started looking for a house. Looking for a house was not as easy as it may seem living in Houston. You have to think about the area you want to buy in, distance to work, traffic, and whether the house would be easy to sell in the future.

George and I finally found the house that we both wanted. It was just perfect for us. The townhouse was beautiful. We wanted the townhouse and we bought it. It is a beautiful two-story, four bed room, and two-car garage townhouse with a beautiful patio in a gated community with only fifty six townhomes. Once we moved in, we started painting the whole interior, bought furniture for the living room and some other odds and ends that we felt we needed or wanted for the house. It is beautiful. I had never lived in such a beautiful house before.

I had never dreamed that I would be living in such a dream home as this. George said he had never lived in a beautiful home like this before, but then he took me to see the "old" houses he lived in when he was growing up and I know different. But it does not matter. For us, the house we live in is a beautiful house and is home and we plan to live here for many years to come, or until we are no longer able to climb the stairs.

George and I knew that we did not want Hanna to have any accidents in the house. So we decided to look into a dog training class. The lady that was assigned to do the training was excellent. We went to Pet Smart and started the training classes. The training was great, except that it was George and I that got trained. We were trained (taught) how to treat a dog. We were taught that we were the masters and she was the dog, instead of the other way around as we had being doing. We were easy to get trained. We did not realize that it was us that had the problem, not Hanna. We just needed to be consistent, let her know what we wanted and expected from her and she was fine. It was so easy.

We taught Hanna not to get on the couch, she let us know when she needed to go out, and we kept her in the cage at night. She had gotten to where she loved her cage. At night when we would start getting ready for bed, she would get in her cage and I would close her door. In the morning, I would take her out to walk and then come in and George had her breakfast ready. We had both gotten to where we enjoyed having Hanna. She was very warm and loving and we loved her very much.

My life with George has been such a blessing. George is extremely intelligent, funny, and he loves to talk. We seem to have so much to talk about. We have done some travelling and I have seen parts of my country that I had wanted to see and some parts that I never, ever thought I would see.

George was born and raised in Chattanooga, Tennessee but lived in Raleigh, North Carolina, for many years. He has traveled to many parts of the United States and the world. It is a pleasure traveling with him because it is like having your own private tour guide. We don't get lost. He made driving in the mountains in North Carolina, easy because he knew where we were going.

I went with George for the first time to Raleigh, North Carolina, to visit his daughter and family.

I got to meet George's son, daughter-in-law, his daughter and son-in-law and his two little granddaughters. His children made me feel very comfortable during our visit and I realized how lucky he was to have this wonderful family. They are very accepting and kind.

It was during Thanksgiving and the weather was cold, foggy and dreary. It was beautiful. I love dreary days. I loved the soft mist in the cold, gray afternoon, the leaves falling, Christmas decorations, the tall trees and the beautiful mountains, simply beautiful.

On one of the mornings, about four o'clock in the morning, the fire alarm sounded in the hotel where we were staying. We were on the second floor and we quickly got dressed and went down the stairs to the outside. There were a lot of people already standing outside. It was freezing cold and a lot of the people had left their rooms without coats or sweaters, only in their pajamas and some were barefooted. After about thirty minutes, we were all told to go back into our rooms. I felt sorry for the people that were barefooted in the cold.

At about an hour later, the fire alarm sounded again. This time when we got to the front door they told us to stay in the lobby while the firemen checked for fire. Some people had said the alarm may have sounded due to someone smoking in the room. This time most of the women had combed their hair, had makeup on and were wearing their shoes and their coats. By this time it was beginning to turn daylight. Employees had made coffee and prepared snacks. All in all, it was a different experience for us. We were glad to be on the second floor instead of the seventh floor though.

Since George and I have being living together, we have gone to San Francisco, Washington DC, North Carolina, South Carolina, Tennessee, and New York. It was a great adventure for me with every city and state that we visited. It was my first time to go to any of those places so it was fascinating for me to see so much for the first time. David and I had planned on traveling to see parts of our country that I wanted to see, but by the time I got to where I had saved enough money to be able to travel, David was not physically able to travel.

Going to Washington D.C., was especially important to me. I have always felt that I was born and raised and live in a great country. I wanted to see the Constitution, the White House, my country's capital, the Washington and Abraham Lincoln monuments and the Arlington National Cemetery. It was emotional for me to be able to see the Constitution. The Constitution protects us, can you imagine that. The Constitution protects me. It took me many years to be able to accomplish my goal to see the Constitution. It was very important and meant so much to me. I hope that every one that lives in this country realizes and appreciates what we have and protects what we have. I have never lived in another country, never been to another country for that matter, but it isn't necessary for me to have lived in another country to appreciate what I have in this country. I feel sad when I realize that I have taken so much for granted.

Being able to be there present at Arlington National Cemetery during the Changing of The Guard was a moving experience for me also. The significance of the Changing of The Guard is very touching. I thought of all the young men and women who have given up their lives for me to have my freedom. I have so much to be grateful and thankful for and I owe it to those who have died for this country, their country and my country.

Going to see the Washington and Abraham Lincoln monuments was a great experience because now I was seeing, first hand, the monuments that I had read about, heard about and seen on television and the movies. I was here seeing it with my own eyes and to top it off, there was a march going on that we had no idea was going to be happening. I saw thousands of people just like they show on television.

George and I went to South Carolina, where I got to meet his mother and his brother, his brother's wife and one of their son's. His mother is very nice and I enjoyed talking, driving to the mountains and going out to eat with her.

We laugh a lot when she and I talk. She has a nice sense of humor. His brother and sister-in-law are nice also.

After we got back from South Carolina we started back into our regular daily routine except that this time Hanna was not doing well. Hanna had been sick for about six months and we had to take her to the veterinary almost every week. She had developed intestinal problems and liver problems. On two different occasions we took her to the animal emergency room. Some days she felt good and she would play with her little toys and then some days she just slept and looked sad. The veterinarian would keep changing medications and running tests on her, but not much was helping her. We changed to a veterinary closer to where we lived and continued running tests and different medications. Nothing seemed to work.

George and I talked about and knew where all this would eventually end. And soon enough, the time came when I had to make that decision. I hated to see Hanna go through pain and to suffer. George and I would get up several times during the night to take Hanna out. She had diarrhea and she let us know when she needed to go. Sometimes I would be sound asleep and I would not hear her barking. George would get up and take her out. Getting her to take her medications had become a hassle. She would cough the pills out and most of the time would not eat. It was time.

George and I both took Hanna to the veterinary and both of us were there until she was brought back to us resting peacefully, without pain. The only other time I had felt this hurt was when David died, and now I was feeling it again. Some people might say she was just a dog, but she was family to me and George. I did not want her ashes, but George and I have beautiful memories that she left us with.

It has been almost a year since we lost Hanna, but George and I still miss her. Every little dog we see, we think of and mention Hanna's name. We have not put away Hanna's toys. I feel putting away her toys is too final. I am not ready yet. She is still here with me. I still talk to her sometimes when I am home alone. When George went to Florida on personal family business, I overslept on two different mornings. Hanna woke me up. I heard her barking and as soon as I woke up, she stopped barking. I thanked her for waking me up as I got out of bed, got ready for work and left the house.

For our first Christmas without her, I used her little toys as Christmas decorations. They looked very pretty. This may sound weird and people will probably think I am just an old man, but I know I am not crazy or lost my mind. I just simply loved my dog.

On George's birthday, we went to New York. For me, it was the first time. I always said I never wanted to go to New York. I have watched "Crime Scene Investigation" on television and I knew I did not care for all the crime and violence in New York. I also heard people say that the people from New York were rude. So I went to New York with George.

George's son lives in Manhattan in New York. We flew to New Jersey, and from there we rode in a limousine to New York. His son had arranged for the limousine to pick us up at the airport and take us to New York. It was a wonderful ride, bumper-to-bumper traffic, at least an hour ride, but I got to see the buildings of New York. I saw The Empire State building in real life for the first time. Wow!

Finally we arrived at the hotel "W" in Manhattan. We were on the sixth floor. We got checked in and George called his son. His son and his wife would be coming to pick us up. In New York, I learned that picking us up did not necessarily mean we would be getting in a car and driving somewhere. We did a lot of walking and a lot of sight-seeing. I got to see the Empire State building up close and at night. And sight-seeing we did.

George's son had planned the whole trip for us and he did a great job. Besides he's celebrating and wanting to make it a great birthday for his father, he also made sure that I got to see as much of New York as I could see in the short time we were there.

I had always wanted to see the Statue of Liberty, and so he planned a boat ride to the island for us to see the Statue. I could not stop staring. The Statue of Liberty was breathtaking, absolutely awesome. I tried to imagine what the people coming in on the ships to America to find or follow their dream would feel when they saw the Statue of Liberty. The Statue of Liberty is a beautiful sight.

We also went to Ellis Island and then on Saturday evening we went to a special restaurant to eat and celebrate George's birthday. This was also New Year's Eve and we walked by Times Square but did not see the "ball drop". We just wanted to see what went on during New Year's Eve in New York. Going to a restaurant to celebrate George's birthday and New Year's Eve is more appropriate for an old man, speaking for myself, than to be partying in large, young people crowds.

I saw so much in four short days. I noticed that New York, was not what I had always thought it would be. I was amazed by the huge number of people walking the streets. Very impressive for me was the way the cars stopped on yellow lights and did not try to run the yellow lights like we do in Houston. Cars quickly stop on yellow lights, but they do drive quite fast. Also the streets are very clean with few homeless people in the streets. I'm sure there are homeless people in New York, but I am just saying that the places we went to and the time we were in New York, I did not see street people. All in all I had a great time. The weather was not cold as I had been told it would be. The people were nice, friendly and helpful.

Coming home, I realized I liked New York. It was fun and I had a wonderful time. New York is not a place where I would like to live, but I can see where young people would enjoy living there. Houston is big enough for me.

I do not know how much more traveling I will do, but I owe George thanks for encouraging me to travel, for being patient and for the love, respect and caring he has shown me. Like I said before, traveling with George is like having my own personal tour guide. He always seems to know where we are going and how to get there.

CHAPTER 35

FOR MY CHILDREN

It has been a long sixty-six years but I can honestly say that it has been a great journey. I thank God for providing me with the strength to carry on when it all would have been easier for me to give up. I set goals for myself and with the force and strength of my Lord, I set out to reach my goals. And even though the road was rough, I can proudly say I have made it. Through the help of so many friends and people that cared, I was able to get away from the cotton fields and the poverty, to living comfortably, happy and looking forward to just enjoying and loving life with George by my side.

I can think of Old Grandfather now and not feel the fear any more. I am grateful for people like Oprah Winfrey that talk about children being sexually abused. Listening to Oprah Winfrey on television made me start thinking about what happened to me and because of her, I decided to get help. I know now that I was not at fault for what Old Grandfather did to me but how could I have known that? How could anyone expect a child to know that they are not at fault? How could I have known that it was not my fault and that I should not have had to carry all the guilt and fear?

I have learned to hold that little boy and assure him that everything is fine, that he is safe and he no longer has to fear. Now I can, and do, hold that little boy each time that those feelings come back to haunt him. Those feelings come much less often, but I still have my moments to where my mind brings back those feelings of worthlessness, feelings of being inferior to others and feelings that I deserve being mistreated. But all I have to do is embrace that little boy and hold him close as I think about what I have accomplished, think of my children, think of all my friends, my new sunrays of solace, and the bad feelings go away. That little boy and I now know that we are safe and no longer have to be afraid. But I do know this, the scars last a lifetime.

I hope that any child that has been or is being abused can find the strength to talk to someone. Parents must maintain a relationship with their children that will make it easy for the child to talk to the parent(s). And most importantly, we, as adults and as parents, must listen. Through the Grace of God, I was able to survive through the entire horrific ordeal and be triumphant. But not everyone that is a victim of abuse is able to be triumphant as I am. I am one of the lucky ones.

As for the hardships that I went through because we were so poor and my having to work starting at age eleven, great, it made me a stronger person. I am glad that I was able to help my Father, able to help pay bills, able to help pay for the old house that we all liked so much, and able to help in whatever other things that had to be paid. It taught me to work hard and provide. I took care of both my parents in their later years and I hope I made their lives easier. My Father taught me to work, my Mother taught me to love and respect people and she taught me that friends are a treasure. My beautiful parents did the best they could for me.

As for my being gay, I do not know or understand why I am like this. It is not something that I "chose" to be, as some people say. I do not remember being asked if I wanted to be gay or straight. I just know that I am who and what I am and it is definitely not by choice. I love my children, my daughter-in-law, and my grandchildren for loving me and accepting me the way I am. I have been so blessed by God to have my children.

I have seen so many changes, so many unbelievable things happen in my lifetime and I am sure there are so many more changes to come that I may or may not get to see. And through these changes some things still remain the same. The most important thing that I have tried not to allow change in my life is the way I have kept God present in my life and I firmly believe that God has Blessed me regardless of who and what I am, and that He loves me unconditionally.

In writing about my life, I am hoping that my children get to know about me, who I am, and where I came from. I hope they do not feel sorry for me, but instead are happy for me and hopefully proud of me. What I want my children and grandchildren to know is that I worked hard and I never gave up wanting to do better.

I always liked school and I have always felt that education is very important in life. I have tried to live by what

I learned from my parents, from my experiences and from people around me. I tried to pick out those things that I saw that worked for other people in a positive way and apply it to my life.

I respected others and was always grateful for what little I had and for what others did for me. I tried to not forget those people that were good to me, that showed kindness to me and that offered their friendships to me. I have never forgotten those people. In my later years, I have made it a point to find those people that were good to me, that offered their help and their friendships and have thanked them.

I know my children and grandchildren know me as a lecturer. That is fine as long as they learn from my lectures. I know I lecture frequently about the importance of education and saving your money. I do lecture maybe a little too much, but it is because I love them and do not want them to go through the hardships that I went through. My lectures are done out of love. If I have influenced my grandchildren to pursue their education, then what more can a grandfather ask for?

I carry beautiful memories of my parents, my children, and my friends that I have treasured throughout my years. My grandchildren have provided me with the most beautiful memories and not a day goes by without me going into my memory bank and think of something or someone that has touched my life in a good way.

I love and am very proud of my daughter, my son, my daughter-in-law, my four grandchildren and two great-granddaughters. I love and think about my daughter that I lost through a miscarriage. Felipe, I am proud of you. You are a hard working man and I hope that you accomplish your dreams. I am happy that you will soon be part of our family.

I love and enjoy all my friends. To my dearest friend David and my beloved dog Hanna, I love you and I miss you. I would not have done it without you.

I am very happy and I am in a place in my life where I can enjoy whatever time George and I may have left. With God in my life, a wonderful man by my side, with my beautiful family and friends, I can easily and proudly say, "I am a success".

One of the greatest joys and proudest moments in my life was reading what Madison, my youngest granddaughter wrote for her school project:

One person I really admire is my grandpa Joe Martinez, His life as a child wasn't very easy, but that never stopped him from following his dreams. He's worked very hard to get where he is today. His family didn't have a lot growing up, and from him I've learned that life is not about what you get but rather about what you give. My grandpa has great perseverance he's not the kind to give up. He tries his best at everything he does and if it's not good enough the first time he'll try again till he gets it right. He taught me to enjoy the simple things in life because they'll become the most important and the things you'll miss the most. He's a very giving person and loves to help others. He's always encouraging me to do my best and reminds me I can do anything I set my mind to. He has the most amazing outlook on life. He enjoys every minute of it and has no regrets. He's always smiling and never fails at making me laugh. His character is incredible and I hope one day I can possess the qualities he has. My grandpa is a very successful person and I'm blessed to have a person like him in my life.

Need I say more?

Made in the USA
Monee, IL
27 April 2022